Lord For All Sea...

Ted Burge is an Emeritus Professor of Physics of the University of London where he was Dean of the Faculty of Science from 1982 to 1986. He obtained his Ph.D at Bristol in 1949 and also studied at Uppsala, Sweden. He is the author of *Atomic Nuclei and their Particles* (Oxford University Press, 2nd edition 1988), and of *Physics on Stamps* (2nd edition, in three volumes 1995, and a fourth volume jointly with Alberto Lumachi 1997, published privately).

In preparation for the Ministry of the Church of England, Ted Burge read theology at Lincoln College, Oxford in 1953. After a year at Cuddesdon Theological College, testing his vocation, he became convinced that his calling was to physics.

Professor Burge is a committed member of the Anglican Church in the parishes of Painswick, Sheepscombe and Cranham in the Diocese of Gloucester.

He is the author of *Lord of All, Hear our Prayer* (Canterbury Press, 1991).

Lord For All Seasons

*Meditative Prayers
on the Lectionary Readings
Years A, B and C*

Ted Burge

Foreword by Bishop David Bentley

CANTERBURY
PRESS
Norwich

© Ted Burge 1998

First published in 1998 by The Canterbury Press Norwich
(a publishing imprint of Hymns Ancient & Modern Limited
a registered charity)
St Mary's Works, St Mary's Plain
Norwich, Norfolk, NR3 3BH

All rights reserved. No part of this publication which is
copyright may be reproduced, stored in a retrieval
system, or transmitted, in any form or by any means,
electronic, mechanical, photocopying, recording, or
otherwise, without the prior permission of the
publisher.

Ted Burge has asserted his right under the Copyright,
Designs and Patents Act, 1988, to be identified as Author
of this Work

British Library Cataloguing in Publication Data

A catalogue record for this book is available
from the British Library

ISBN 1-85311-221-6

Typeset by Rowland Phototypesetting Ltd
printed in Great Britain by
Biddles Ltd, Guildford and King's Lynn

Contents

Lord for All Seasons

Advent

Christmas

Epiphany *(RCL = Ordinary Time)*

Ordinary Time

Lent

Easter

Ordinary Time *(RCL = The Season after Pentecost)*

Sundays after Trinity

Foreword

by the Rt Revd David Bentley, Bishop of Gloucester

The value of these meditative prayers for private use lies not least in what has shaped them. They are the fruits of much reflection by Professor Ted Burge on the recently authorized Scripture readings for the Eucharist. They are a resource for personal devotion, but they are also anchored in the central act of Christian worship by which the Church is constantly being refreshed and renewed.

The importance of preparing ourselves before coming to the Eucharist cannot be overestimated. The reading of the Scripture passages beforehand, and the offering of these meditative prayers based upon them, can help us to engage in the Eucharist with a greater sense of expectation. They will serve no less to keep us spiritually focused where there are spaces in the liturgy for private reflection and prayer. Many people will also find in here a source of continuing nourishment as they ponder on the significance for their daily lives of what they have heard and received in the Eucharist.

The words and phrases used in this fertile resource have been chosen with great care. Skill and sensitivity are evident in the choices made, and the results are meditative prayers which convey something of what we might want to say to God in the light of his saving acts. Even more importantly, taken with the readings to which they are linked, they can also alert us to what God might be wanting to say to us.

What makes this compilation especially welcome is that the author is a devout Christian layman whose professional background in science enables him to understand the prevailing culture of our times. Professor Burge has done us a great service in what he has compiled. I commend his offering very warmly and greatly look forward to making good use of it in my own spiritual life.

Eastertide 1998

Preface

The Revised Common Lectionary (referred to as the RCL or RCL 1992) has had a considerable influence on the lectionaries adopted by a wide range of churches. The Lectionary recently authorized by the Church of England is published in *The Christian Year: Calendar, Lectionary and Collects* (referred to as CLC or CLC 2000), and is closely similar to the RCL.

The provision of commentaries on the readings for the principal service is helpful not only for those who prepare sermons but also for those who like to prepare for worship or to follow up the service with study in their homes. For Year C, first used in 1997–8, there is the commentary *Word of Life* written by Martin Kitchen, Georgiana Heskins and Stephen Motyer, published by Canterbury Press. *Word of Promise* has recently been published for Year A and *Word of Truth* is due for Year B.

Another need is for assistance in relating intercessions to the readings, and help has been provided in Raymond Chapman's book *Leading Intercessions*, also published by Canterbury Press. This covers all three years of the new Lectionary.

Private prayer and meditation relating to the readings are not easy for most people, and I have aimed to provide some help by using the readings at the principal service for a given Sunday or Festival to write a prayer that covers most of the selected passages. The prayers can be used as preparation for worship, or during worship in times of quiet, or in later reflection in the home. Although the new Lectionary does not provide an explicit theme for each Sunday, as did the ASB 1980, it is often possible to identify the unity in the four selected passages, and this is particularly true for the Principal Feasts. For other Sundays, these prayers attempt to draw together the readings into a single act of encounter with God, with elements of praise, confession, resolution and hope-filled expressions of trust and worship.

In writing these prayers, I have studied the readings in at least two versions, one of which is the recommended New Revised Standard Version of the Bible. Significant phrases, images and thoughts have been identified for weaving into the final prayer. I have been impressed once again by the power of many of the Psalms and have enjoyed the freshness of their phrases, which fit so well into New Testament contexts. In general, the actual words of one or other of the translations have been incorporated directly into the prayers, even when they sound a little old-fashioned or tied to the localities and times of the writers. The result serves to remind us of the continuing development of God's revelation. Some translations vary the familiar phrases of well-loved passages and, where these help to make more vivid the meaning of the thoughts, I have not hesitated to use them. In attempting to discover the divine message in narratives of events, the stories have sometimes been rehearsed as if God is present and paying attention – as I feel sure he is. There seems to be a specially powerful effect in so doing, that brings to life and meaning what can otherwise be difficult passages.

Some of the Principal Feasts, Principal Holy Days and related days are assigned identical or closely parallel readings for all three years. Only one prayer is then provided and is to be found in Year A (with 'Years A, B and C' under the heading). Sundays between 29 May and 29 October (the Sundays after Trinity) are provided with alternative Old Testament readings called 'Continuous' and 'Related', the former providing a partly continuous reading of certain books, the latter providing passages selected to relate directly to the New Testament readings. For each of these Sundays, only one prayer is given, covering six rather than four readings.

Where the needs of the RCL differ from those of the Church of England Lectionary, provision has been made for extra prayers. This book therefore should be of interest not only to members of the Church of England but also to those who use the RCL or closely similar lectionaries.

Introduction to the Revised Common Lectionary and the new Lectionary of the Church of England

The new Lectionary of the Church of England was published in 1997 under the title *The Christian Year: Calendar, Lectionary and Collects* (CLC or CLC 2000), and included Post Communion Prayers and a Commentary with Sources. The Lectionary is closely similar to the Revised Common Lectionary of 1992 (the RCL). The RCL was prepared by the Consultation on Common Texts, a body which was formed in the mid-1960s in the United States and Canada and which now includes Roman Catholics and a wide range of Protestant denominations and churches all over the world.

The very title 'Revised Common Lectionary' indicates that there was an earlier 'Common Lectionary'. This was published in 1983 as an ecumenical lectionary and was adopted by a number of Anglican Provinces, including the USA and Canada. It was based on the Roman Catholic Lectionary of 1969, one of the fruits of the Second Vatican Council (1963), which is now used throughout the world in 400 different languages and has definitively influenced subsequent lectionaries. The importance of the word 'Common' in the title 'Revised Common Lectionary' can scarcely be over-emphasized. The RCL is a great achievement with real spiritual significance, in that so many churches throughout the world now use almost identical sets of readings Sunday by Sunday and on Feasts and Festivals.

In the CLC, readings are provided for the principal Sunday service using a three-year cycle – Years A, B and C. When the year (e.g. 1998) is exactly divisible by three ($1998 \div 3 = 666$), the readings from Advent (1998) are for Year A. There are four readings: one from the Old Testament, including the Apocrypha; one from the Psalms; one from the New Testament Apostolic Writings; and one from the Gospels. In each year, one of the Synoptic Gospels (i.e. Matthew, Mark and Luke) predominates, aiming at a continuous approach to reading it. St John's Gospel is spread through every year. Other books are also read in a partly continuous way. The Acts of the Apostles is the first reading in Eastertide, but there is an Old Testament alternative reading for these eight Sundays and for Ascension Day.

The Sundays after Trinity between 29 May and 29 October are now named Proper 4 to Proper 25, as in the RCL. They are correlated in the Table on page 208 for the years from 1999 to 2018, giving the Year (A, B or C), the date of the First Sunday after Trinity, and the corresponding Proper for that Sunday. Numbered Sundays after Trinity will be retained in most churches. Propers 4 to 25 are provided with alternatives for the Old Testament and Psalms. One alternative for these Sundays is named 'Continuous' and aims to follow through the books in a partly continuous way, while the other is named 'Related' and provides readings that are directly related to the New Testament readings. It is intended that, for a given year, either 'Continuous' or 'Related' should be adhered to by a given congregation.

Small changes in the names of Sundays occur, all for good reasons. For example, we now have Sundays 'of' Christmas, Epiphany and Easter, rather than Sundays 'after', because they are clearly part of those Seasons. Thus we have 'The Second Sunday of Easter' instead of the 'Easter 1' of the ASB. But 'after' is right, and therefore retained, for 'weekdays after Pentecost' and 'Sundays after Trinity'.

In the new Lectionary (CLC), as well as the readings for the principal Sunday service, there are revised provisions for the Principal Feasts, Principal Holy Days, Festivals and Lesser Festivals and Special Occasions. Names of individuals have been added for Lesser Festivals, reflecting a fairly conservative approach to Anglican divines and saintly people of the last two centuries.

Readings are also provided in the CLC for a Second Service, which in many communities will be the Sunday evening service, and a Third Service, meeting the need for a Sunday Office lectionary as at Morning Prayer. These Second and Third Services are absent from the RCL.

Where the 1662 Book of Common Prayer Communion Service is used, the BCP Epistle and Gospel are allowed.

The themes given in the ASB 1980 (page 1092) have been dropped, by common consent. It is clear that Seasons and certain Sundays provide their own themes, but there is no predetermined list. Nevertheless, themes emerge from every creative engagement with Scripture and are to be found occasionally (without being over-emphasized) in the prayers of this book.

The CLC and the RCL are so close that it was decided to make this book equally suitable for both. The Church of England has added four occasions to the RCL list: Christmas Eve, Mothering Sunday, Bible

Sunday and Dedication Sunday. The CLC omits two occasions from the RCL: New Year's Day (1 January) and Easter Evening. There are variations in the names of Sundays and Holy Days (see the Contents list, pages v–viii), and there are different readings for the Second Sunday before Lent in the CLC, which is called the Eighth Sunday after Epiphany in the RCL. The addition in this book of six prayers to those provided for the CLC covers the need for the extra prayers for the RCL. There are a number of minor variations in the readings and in the verses selected for a given reading. The references for readings given here are, where possible, from the CLC.

There are a few differences worth mentioning between the Roman Lectionary and both the RCL and the CLC. During the Sundays after Trinity the Roman Lectionary does not have an alternative Old Testament track. Where the Roman Lectionary provides a reading from the Apocrypha, the RCL and the CLC provide a canonical alternative. Quite a number of verses are omitted from readings in the Roman Lectionary, and in the RCL these are either restored or are added as options in brackets.

This great forward-looking enterprise, already in use in many communions, was launched in the Church of England at Advent 1997 (Year C). As well as providing readings that follow closely the deeply considered principles agreed by a wide variety of persuasions, it will also generate a clearly visible ecumenical pattern of worship uniting the spiritual needs of all Christians.

Acknowledgements

For their interest, support and a goodly number of comments, I am indebted to Sarah James, the Revd Peter Minall and Eileen Cottle of Painswick. My wife, Elizabeth, has been particularly patient and helpful and has added a number of most perceptive comments.

Permission to use material from *The Christian Year: Calendar, Lectionary and Collects* (Church House Publishing, 1997) has been kindly granted by The Central Board of Finance of the Church of England.

Permission to use material from *The Revised Common Lectionary* (© 1992) has been kindly granted by the Consultation on Common Texts (CCT), PO Box 840, Room 381, Nashville, TN 37202−0840, USA.

Lord For All Seasons

Year A

The First Sunday of Advent

Isaiah 2:1–5; Psalm 122; Romans 13:11–14; Matthew 24:36–44.

Lord for the Season of Advent,
   enliven our expectation
     of your coming,
and prepare us for the adventures
   of our spiritual pilgrimage.

Year by year we celebrate
   the coming of Jesus,
and live again the past,
   recapitulating events
     foretold by the prophets.

We prepare for the feast of Christmas,
   taking care to present gifts that please
     to family and friends.

Let our Advent prayers,
   and our meditations on the future,
     be given as much attention
       as our Christmas greetings,
         and the presents we select.

Grant that our foremost desires shall be
   to love you with heart and mind and soul,
     and to enrich our devotion daily
       by worship and thanksgiving.

We know not the day or the hour of your coming,
   nor the manner of the surprise –
     two men in a field, one is taken;
     two women grinding at the mill, one is taken;
       like a house being broken into.

Wake us from the slumber of habit,
   that we may cast off the deeds of darkness,
and be defended by the armour of light,
   which is Jesus Christ our Saviour.

The Second Sunday of Advent

Isaiah 11:1–10; Psalm 72:1–7, 18–19 (*or* Psalm 72:1–7); Romans 15:4–13; Matthew 3:1–12.

Lord of our hope,
   sown by the prophets,
      fed and watered by worship and faith,
         harvested in your birth to Mary.

Longed-for king, cradled in creation,
   symbolically to be anointed with oil,
      the token of joy and glory,
   and to wear the royal belt of justice,
   and to be girdled with divine truth,
on whom would rest
   the Spirit of wisdom and understanding,
   the Spirit of counsel and power,
   and of knowledge and fear of God.

We prepare ourselves, as we remember you,
   to bring relief to the oppressed,
   and provisions for the needy,
      for the kingdom of heaven is upon us,
        calling us to repentance,
           and love of our neighbour.

Scriptures written long ago
   expressed a yearning for a new age,
   and by their instruction and encouragement
      people maintained then, and do now maintain,
        hope with perseverance.

Help us, Lord, to prepare the way for you,
   by crying out in the wilderness
      of this world's longing and despair,
   and by leading a life of faith,
      filled with all joy and peace,
until by the power of the Holy Spirit
   we overflow with trust and hope and love,
   and attract others to your keeping.

The Third Sunday of Advent

Isaiah 35:1–10; Psalm 146:5–10 (*or Canticle*: Magnificat); James 5:7–10; Matthew 11:2–11.

Lord for all time,
  time past, time present,
  and both the near and distant future,
renew in our hearts and minds
  the message of John the Baptist.

He prepared a way for you,
  heralding miraculous transformations,
    from sickness to health,
    from blindness to sight,
    and from death to life.

You prepared for us the Way of Holiness,
  the pilgrim's way, along which we follow you,
    as devoted disciples.

Inspire us with Mary's vision
  of the kingdom of heaven on earth,
    loving others more than self,
    filling the hungry with good things,
    declaring good news to the poor,
    welcoming strangers in our land,
    and praising God in his glory.

Help us to follow the pattern of patience
  lived out by the prophets, in spite of ill-treatment.

Make us, like them, stout-hearted in disappointment,
  and determined to try again
    when failure seems to be our lot.

In the deserts of our emptiness
  let the mirage become a pool,
and in the wilderness of our unworthiness
  let waters spring up to cleanse us and refresh us,
so that we may embrace the future
  with outstanding trust and unlimited hope.

The Fourth Sunday of Advent

Isaiah 7:10–16; Psalm 80:1–7, 17–19 (*or* Psalm 80:1–7); Romans 1:1–7;
Matthew 1:18–25.

Lord of the patience
   that never wears out
      when your people are obtuse,
         and obstinate,
         and disobedient,

As the shepherd of Israel,
   you came to their rescue and restored them,
      that they might be saved,
         and given new life,
            by calling on your name.

By the prophets, in sacred Scriptures,
   the gospel was announced beforehand,
      good news for all the nations,
      the gospel of Jesus,
         Emmanuel,
         God with us.

As man, Jesus was a descendant of David,
   but on the plane of the Holy Spirit
      he was declared Son of God,
         by the act of power
            that raised him from the dead.

Grant us the measure of trust and patience
   that Joseph enjoyed in Mary
      when he was told by an angel in a dream
         that her conception
            was through the Holy Spirit.

May the same Holy Spirit
   enable us to be conceived again,
      and born again,
         through faith in Jesus.

Christmas Eve

Years A, B and C.

2 Samuel 7:1–5, 8–11, 16; Psalm 89:2, 21–27; Acts 13:16–26; Luke 1:67–79.

Lord, the God of Israel,
    content in the time of David
        for the Ark of God to be housed in a tent,

You trusted Solomon to build you a Temple,
    promising never to withdraw your love from him.

With his message of repentance and baptism,
    John, Prophet of the Most High,
        realised that after him came one with a message of salvation,
        whose sandals he was not worthy to unfasten.

As we wait to celebrate the birthday of Jesus,
    we join in the Spirit-filled prophecy of Zechariah:
        'Praise to the Lord, the God of Israel,
            for he has turned to his people and set them free.
        He has raised for us a strong deliverer
            from the house of his servant David.
        So he promised; age after age he proclaimed,
            that he would deliver us,
                calling to mind his solemn covenant.
        This was the oath he swore to our father Abraham,
            so that we might worship in his presence,
                in holiness and righteousness our whole life long.
        You, my child, will be the Lord's forerunner,
            to prepare his way, and lead his people
                to a knowledge of salvation,
                    through the forgiveness of their sins.
    For in the tender compassion of our God
        the dawn from heaven will break upon us,
            to shine on those who live in darkness,
                and to guide our feet into the way of peace.'

7

Christmas Day (I)

Years A, B and C. 25 December.

Any of the sets of reading (I), (II) and (III) may be used on the evening of Christmas Eve and on Christmas Day.

Isaiah 9:2–7; Psalm 96; Titus 2:11–14; Luke 2:1–14, [15–20].

Lord our deliverer,
   Messiah and king, Prince of Peace,

we rejoice on this your birthday,
   like those who rejoice at harvest,
      knowing that your zeal, the zeal of the Lord of Hosts,
         will lead us to boundless peace.

We sing a new song and bless your name,
   declaring your glory among the nations,
      sensing in the sanctuary of a manger
         your majesty and splendour, your might and beauty.

Your grace has dawned upon the world
   with healing for all mankind,
      and with discipline to renounce
         godless ways and worldly desires.

Shepherds in the fields, keeping watch throughout the night,
   were terrified by an angel,
      who said, as angels often say, 'Do not be afraid.'

The good news of the angel
   told of your birth as the Messiah, the Lord,
      in a Bethlehem stable with a manger as a cradle,
         for there was no room in the inn.

Mary, at peace, as one that is highly favoured,
   treasured the message of the angel,
      and pondered these things in her heart.

Grant us grace that we may do likewise.

Christmas Day (II)

Years A, B and C. 25 December.

Isaiah 62:6–12; Psalm 97; Titus 3:4–7; Luke 2:[1–7,] 8–20.

Lord who became King,
    with righteousness and justice
        as the foundation of your throne,

You took no rest until Jerusalem was made renowned,
    a theme of praise throughout the world,
        and renamed 'City No Longer Forsaken'.

Those who garnered grain did eat the bread,
    and those who gathered grapes did drink the wine,
        remembering the Lord within his sacred courts.

A highway was built for the arrival of the deliverer,
    a harvest of light for the righteous,
        and joy for the upright in heart.

In Jesus our Saviour our deliverer has come,
    your kindness and generosity have dawned upon the world,
    the renewing power of the Holy Spirit has been lavished upon us,
so that, justified by grace, we might become heirs to eternal life.

You speak to us as you spoke to the shepherds, by an angel,
    calming our fear and terror, promising a sign,
a babe in a manger, wrapped in swaddling bands of cloth,
    Messiah and Lord.

And we too marvel at the song of the heavenly host,
    'Glory to God in highest heaven,
        and on earth peace, to all in whom he delights.'

Help us to follow the wisdom of Mary,
    as we treasure the identity of the infant Messiah,
        and ponder in our hearts
            the cost of peace on earth.

Christmas Day (III)

Years A, B and C. 25 December.

*These readings should be used at some service during the celebration of
Christmas Day.*

Isaiah 52:7–10; Psalm 98; Hebrews 1:1–4, [5–12]; John 1:1–14.

Lord in the beginning,
   Word that already was, in God's presence,
      and what God was, you were.

Through you all things came to be,
   in you was life, the light of mankind,
      testified to by John who was not that light,
      you were a light shining in the darkness
         that could not overcome you.

John bore witness to your true light
   and the world did not recognize you.

But to those who trusted in you
   you gave the right and power
      to become the children of God.

So you, the Word, became flesh,
   and we saw your glory,
   such glory as befits the Father's only Son,
      full of grace and truth.

How beautiful on the mountains
   are the feet of the herald bringing the good news
      that the whole world shall see
         the deliverance wrought by our God.

You are the radiance of God's glory,
   sustaining the universe by the word of your power,
      anointed with oil, the token of joy.
With you, by your grace, we too rejoice.

The First Sunday of Christmas

Isaiah 63:7–9; Psalm 148:1–14 (*or* Psalm 148:7–14); Hebrews 2:10–18;
Matthew 2:13–23.

Lord of the family, of its wholeness, and its parts,
you did not shrink from becoming brother to us all,
  so that we might share in your divine nature.

You liberated those who all their life
    had been in servitude,
      through fear of death.

By passing through the test of suffering,
  you are able to help
    those in the midst of suffering,
      as the pioneer of their salvation.

Even when your people rebelled,
  you trusted them as children not to play you false,
and by your tenderness,
  and many acts of faithful love,
    you delivered them in their troubles.

Kings and commoners praise your name,
  old and young together,
    for you have exalted their souls,
      in the pride of your power.

By that same power
  bind together our families with your brotherly love,
  and nurture and tutor our faith and hope.

Weave into our worship the significance
  of the flight into Egypt,
  the massacre of the innocents,
  the return to Israel,
  and the settlement in Nazareth.

Give grace to families under threat.

The Second Sunday of Christmas

Jeremiah 31:7–14; Psalm 147:12–20 (*or* Ecclesiasticus 24:1–12; *Canticle*: Wisdom of Solomon 10:15–21); Ephesians 1:3–14; John 1:[1–9,] 10–18.

Lord of all grace and truth,
   mediated through Jesus Christ,
      who became man,
         in every respect as we are,
            and made his home among us,
               taking root among his people,

We glory in your presence,
   and thank you for all we have received,
      from your full store of grace upon grace.

To those who accept you,
   and trust you,
      you have given the right to become
         your adopted children,
            united in Christ.

Their sorrow will be turned into joy,
   their grief into gladness,
      and they will become radiant
         when they see the bounty of the Lord.

By your will and pleasure,
   you confer on them every spiritual blessing,
that the glory of your gracious gift
   might redound to your praise.

In the richness of your grace,
   lavish on us a wealth
      of wisdom and insight,
and stamp us with the seal
   of the promised Holy Spirit,
      the pledge of our inheritance.

The Epiphany

Years A, B and C. 6 January.

Isaiah 60:1–6; Psalm 72:[1–9,] 10–15; Ephesians 3:1–12; Matthew 2:1–12.

Lord of all the nations,
  you manifest your glory
    to both Gentiles and Jews.

Convinced of the imminence of a royal birth,
  astrologers from the East
    journeyed to Jerusalem,
      to find the new-born King of the Jews.

Chief priests and scribes were already convinced
  that out of Bethlehem would come a King
    to be the shepherd of Israel.

Lord, you were more than an earthly king,
  more than a shepherd of Israel,
for you were God incarnate,
  Saviour of all the nations.

The gifted Gentiles from the East
  symbolize for us the seekers of all the ages,
    overjoyed in their discovery,
      paying homage with their gold,
      worshipping with frankincense,
      foretelling mystery with myrrh.

Grant us, Lord, to recognize more clearly
  whom we sought when you sought us,
  and whom we found when you found us,
    so that we discover anew
      the unfathomable riches
        of Jesus Christ, our Saviour.

The Baptism of Christ

The First Sunday of Epiphany.

Isaiah 42:1–9; Psalm 29; Acts 10:34–43; Matthew 3:13–17.

Lord of humility,
    obedience and purity,
    baptized by John because it is right
      to do all that God requires,

Your baptism was with the Holy Spirit,
   confirmed by the voice from heaven,
     'This is my beloved Son, in whom I take delight.'

The earlier prophecies had come to pass,
   and now you declared new things,
     the tidings of the kingdom of heaven,
      salvation for all the nations.

You taught us that God has no favourites,
   for in every nation
     those who are God-fearing
      and do what is right,
        are acceptable to God.

God raised you from the dead,
   clearly seen by chosen witnesses,
     with whom you ate and drank
      after your resurrection.

Enrich us in the continual renewing of that remembrance,
   when we eat and drink with you
     as one body.

By the mystery of your Spirit
   use our witness to convince others
     of restoration and renewal,
     and of loving forgiveness,
      through and in your name.

The Second Sunday of Epiphany

Isaiah 49:1–7; Psalm 40:1–11; 1 Corinthians 1:1–9; John 1:29–42.

Lord, you listen to our cry,
  when it seems we toil in vain,
    and spend our strength for nothing,
      and to no purpose.

We know our cause is with you,
  and our desire is to do your will,
    with your law in our heart.

Set our feet on rock,
  give us a firm foothold,
    and help us to proclaim in a new song
      your faithfulness and saving power,
      your unfailing love and truth.

You are a light to all the nations,
  and your salvation reaches Earth's farthest bounds,
    for you are God's chosen one
      whom all may come and see.

John, with his baptismal zeal,
  recognized you as the Lamb of God,
    to be a sacrifice for sin,
      and to baptize with the fire of the Spirit.

You invited disciples to your dwelling, saying, 'Come and see,'
  and the first thing Andrew did was to bring his brother, Simon,
    whom you named Peter, the Rock,
      and they knew they had found the Messiah.

May grace and peace dwell with us,
  and may your enrichment of our lives,
    through the power of the gospel,
      enable others to see in us
        evidence for the truth of Christ.

The Third Sunday of Epiphany

Isaiah 9:1–4; Psalm 27:1, 4–9 (*or* Psalm 27:1–9). 1 Corinthians 1:10–18;
Matthew 4:12–23.

Lord of the oneness of unity,
   Christ is not divided,
      but we are, in denominational disarray,
         in spite of being members
            of the kingdom of heaven.

Grant us the gift of toleration
   of the beliefs and practices of all your children,
      with determination to understand
         when we are able to converse,
      and a willingness to experience
         varieties of ritual.

Above all, grant us a sense
   of common relation to you,
      and of the healing power of your Spirit.

In days of darkness,
   and in places as dark as death,
      the light of your salvation is radiance divine,
and in times of despair and misfortune
   you will hide us in your shelter,
      and never reject or forsake us,
         when we seek your presence.

Those who do not fathom the message of the cross
   see it as sheer and utter folly,
but those who repent and believe
   and are on the way to salvation
      see it as the mystery of divine power.

Heal us of our infirmities of mind and heart and soul
   and use us to proclaim your message
      as we thrust out into the deep,
         casting our nets on the right side,
            to become your fishers of men and women.

The Fourth Sunday of Epiphany

1 Kings 17:8–16; Psalm 36:5–10; 1 Corinthians 1:18–31; John 2:1–11.

God of all wisdom,
　　you made worldly wisdom foolish
　　　　and showed your divine wisdom
　　　　　　in the power of Christ.

You chose what the world counted as weakness
　　to put to shame the pride of the strong,
　　　　for there is no need for human pride
　　　　　　in the presence of the divine.

The Jews sought for signs,
　　and you gave them in abundance,
　　　　more than they could understand.

The Greeks looked for wisdom,
　　and you gave of the wisdom of the world,
　　　　preparing the way
　　　　　　from worship of their unknown God
　　　　　　　　to the love of Jesus.

The food of faith, like the widow's store,
　　does not run out,
nor yet the wine of the bride and groom,
　　the Church and Christ,
provided we do whatever you tell us,
　　as Mary told the servants at the wedding.

Your unfailing love and faithfulness
　　reach to the heavens,
your righteousness is like the highest mountains,
your justice like the deepest of the seas.

You give frail humans to drink
　　from the streams of your delights,
　　　　for with you is the fountain of life,
and you continue to give your saving power
　　to the honest of heart,
　　　　who respond with the outpouring of thanks and praise.

The Presentation of Christ in the Temple

Years A, B and C. Candlemas, 2 February.

Malachi 3:1–5; Psalm 24:[1–6,] 7–10; Hebrews 2:14–18; Luke 2:22–40.

Lord God of Hosts,
    and King of Glory,

every firstborn was deemed by the law to belong to you,
    and Mary's firstborn, Jesus,
        was obediently brought to the Temple
and recognized as restorer of Israel, promised Messiah,
    by aged Simeon,
        upright and devout, watching and waiting.

Simeon saw what lay ahead –
    rejection for Jesus,
    heart-piercing sorrow for Mary,
        and for many the laying bare of their secret thoughts.

Jesus grew big and strong, enriched by many friends,
    in uncanny rapport with his companions,
    full of wisdom, and with your favour upon him.

He went up to the mountain of the Lord,
    and stood in the holy place,
    a priest, yet not ordained,
    a prophet in his teens.
He had clean hands and a pure heart,
    and set not his mind on what was false,
        nor yet swore deceitfully.

For him the Temple gates lifted up their heads,
    for the King of Glory to come in.

May we recognize him, with you, Lord, as the King of Glory,
    the eternal, majestic, Lord of Hosts,
        mighty in the battle with evil,
            triumphant in resurrection.

Proper 1

The Sunday between 3 and 9 February inclusive (if earlier than the Second Sunday before Lent).

Isaiah 58:1–9a, [9b–12]; Psalm 112:1–9, [10]; 1 Corinthians 2:1–12, [13–16]; Matthew 5:13–20.

Lord for all Seasons,
    for Festivals and Holy Days, and for Ordinary Time,
you are timeless in eternity,
    and eternal in perpetuity.

You have made clear the fast you require,
    the setting free of the oppressed, sharing food with the hungry,
    taking the homeless poor into our home, fulfilling our duty to kinsfolk,
        so that when we call, Lord, you will answer.

When we fear you, with love and trust,
    we find deep delight in obeying your commandments,
news of misfortunes has no terrors for us,
    because our hearts are steadfast,
    and in honour we carry our heads high.

The gospel carries conviction by its spiritual power,
    and penetrating arguments have no place
        except they be with the spiritual wisdom of your secret purpose
        to bring us to our destined glory.

By the Spirit we explore everything,
    even the depths of your very nature,
        and the mind of Christ.

You have prepared for those who love you
    things beyond our seeing,
    things beyond our hearing,
    things beyond our imagination,
        all to be judged in the light of the Spirit.

Grant that we may shed light among our neighbours,
    when they see us obeying your commandments,
        so that they may be led to do likewise,
        giving praise to you for enabling grace.

Proper 2

The Sunday between 10 and 16 February inclusive (if earlier than the Second Sunday before Lent).

Deuteronomy 30:15–20 (*or* Ecclesiasticus 15:15–20); Psalm 119:1–8; 1 Corinthians 3:1–9; Matthew 5:21–37.

Lord, you demand
   that we choose between good and evil,
      between life and death,
      between blessing and curse.

Enter our hearts and let us be so minded
   that we turn not away,
      fail to listen, and so perish.

Lift us from the merely natural plane,
   the purely human level, with its jealousy and strife,
      to the spiritual plane of loving communion.

Feed us with the solid food of your instruction,
   that we may grow like well-watered plants in your garden.

Keep us aware of the dangers
   of anger nursed against our neighbours,
      or by our neighbours.

If we suddenly remember a grievance held against us,
   give us the grace and courage
      to make peace with the grieved
         before we offer gifts at your altar.

Guard us against the lust in our heart
   that amounts already to adultery.

Give us a simple approach to honesty,
   with unembroidered 'Yes' and 'No',
      lest our qualifications and additions be deviously evil.

Above all let us realise that a plain 'Yes',
   in answer to your call,
      is all we need for salvation.

Proper 3

The Sunday between 17 and 23 February inclusive (if earlier than the Second Sunday before Lent).

Leviticus 19:1–2, 9–18; Psalm 119:33–40. 1 Corinthians 3:10–11, 16–23; Matthew 5:38–48.

Lord of all holiness and goodness,
   help us to be holy,
      and let there be no limit to our goodness.

Help us to be generous to the poor
   and welcome strangers in community,
      never to cheat or deceive our neighbour or oppress or rob him,
      never to nurse hatred towards our brother,
      never to seek revenge or cherish a grudge,
      never to treat the deaf with contempt,
   nor put obstacles in the way of the blind,
      and always to administer justice with the strictest fairness.

You have revised the law of revenge
   and commanded us to love our enemies,
      and to pray for our persecutors.

Only if we love our neighbour as ourselves
   can we truly become your children.

You cause the sun to shine, and the rain to fall,
   on good and bad alike.

The whole order of the physical universe, by your will and design,
   treats all people with consistency,
so that we know that we can trust you,
   use trustworthiness as a basis for love,
      and feel free to choose with foresight
         between good and evil,
            in the power of the Spirit.

For order and beauty, we thank you, God.

The Second Sunday before Lent

Genesis 1:1 – 2:3; Psalm 136:1–26 (*or* Psalm 136:1–9, 23–26); Romans 8:18–25; Matthew 6:25–34.

Lord of all, seen and unseen,
  by your creative power and revelation,
    the stars and planets served as signs,
      for festivals, seasons and years.

By the seed of plants, and of animals,
  living creatures exercised their fruitfulness
    and multiplied in great variety.

Mankind evolved, and still evolves,
  in your image, and in your likeness,
    and has dominion and responsibility over living creatures.

You remembered your chosen nation,
  when their fortunes were low,
    and rescued them from their enemies,
      for they trusted in you.

Witnesses to the gospel of Jesus endured many sufferings,
    but declared they bore no comparison
      with the glory in store for them,
when the universe will be freed from the shackles of mortality,
  and they enter the glorious liberty of your children.

Grant that we may cast aside all anxiety
  about food and drink and clothes,
    for you, Lord, know we have need of all those things,
      and there are more important things in life.

Help us to set our minds on your kingdom,
  and on your justice and peace
    before anything else,
knowing that the rest will follow,
  with tomorrow looking after itself,
    each day having troubles enough,
through which we live by grace,
  and give thanks for your enduring love.

Eighth Sunday after the Epiphany

RCL: Year A. Equivalent of the Second Sunday before Lent of CLC.

Isaiah 49:8–16a; Psalm 131; 1 Corinthians 4:1–5; Matthew 6:24–34.

Lord, you are our judge,
    so we must pass no premature judgements,
        but await your disclosure of our inward motives.

No one can serve two masters,
    for he will be devoted to one and hate and despise the other,
        not least when the masters are you and wealth.

How dare Israel say that you had forsaken them,
    as if a woman could forget the infant at her breast,
        or a mother the child in her womb;
and even if these could forget, yet you would never forget.

There were those whose hearts were not proud,
    nor were their eyes haughty.
May we learn from them and not busy ourselves
    with things too great or marvellous for us,
        but calm and quiet our souls
            like a weaned child clinging to its mother.

Take from us all anxious and faithless thoughts
    concerning things material – food, drink and clothes –
        for you know we need them all.
Grant us the quality of faith shown by your care
    for the birds that do not sow, reap or store in barns,
    and for the lilies of the field that do not work or spin
        yet would be, in their splendour, the envy of Solomon.

Lord for all seasons,
    let the rhythms of nature
        and the varieties of its wonders
            lift our hearts and minds to praise your name.

The Sunday next before Lent

Exodus 24:12−18; Psalm 2 (*or* Psalm 99); 2 Peter 1:16−21; Matthew 17:1−9.

Lord of the transfiguration
    of the minds and hearts of mankind,
        from the murky darkness of self-centredness
        to the daybreak of healthy self-abandon,
            with its morning star
                illuminating our whole being,

Draw us to you on the mountain,
    to stay there, like Moses,
        forty days and forty nights
            covered by the cloud of your knowing,
and then descend with your commandments,
    inscribed not only on tablets of stone,
        but on our far from stony hearts.

You are a God of forgiveness,
    yet you call us to account
        for our misdeeds,
            and we bow down at your footstool.

You confirm for us the message of the prophets,
    which goes on shining
        like a lamp in a dark place,
            and is not to be a matter
                for private interpretation.

Your power in Jesus is made known to us
    in the conversion of our wills
        and in the rebirth of our consciences,
reinforcing the witness
    of those who saw with their own eyes
        the majesty of Jesus,
            and heard his command,
                'Stand up,
                    and do not be afraid.'

Ash Wednesday

Years A, B and C.

Joel 2:1–2, 12–17 (*or* Isaiah 58:1–12); Psalm 51:1–17; 2 Corinthians
5:20b – 6:10; Matthew 6:1–6, 16–21 (*or* John 8:1–11).

Lord our deliverer,
   your righteousness is our vanguard,
      and your glory our rearguard.

You rebuild the broken walls of our resolve,
   and restore the ruined houses of our hopes.

Your light bursts upon us like the dawn,
   we are washed and made whiter than snow,
      restored to the joy of your deliverance,
         and upheld by your willing and steadfast Spirit.

You desire faithfulness in our inmost beings,
   and tutored wisdom in our hearts,
so that we avoid giving offence in anything
   by our steadfast endurance, innocent behaviour,
      patience and kindliness,
   and by our grasp of the truth
      as we live the spiritual life of unaffected love.

In this season of abstinence,
   let us not indulge in the mortification
      that leads to wrangling and strife,
         serving only our own interests,
nor wear the gloomy look of the hypocrite,
   reinforcing in others the common misapprehension of fasting.

Encourage us, instead, to wash our faces
   and show no mourning in our dress,
      so that no one knows that we are fasting.

Inspire us to rend our hearts and not our garments,
   to live by the discipline of suffering,
   to find cause for joy in our sorrows,
   and bring true wealth to others
      by abandoning the false riches of this world.

The First Sunday of Lent

Genesis 2:15–17; 3:1–7; Psalm 32; Romans 5:12–19; Matthew 4:1–11.

Lord for all the seasons of creation,
   throughout the space and time
     of the evolving universe,
   help us to discover the fullness
     of the knowledge of right and wrong.

By observation, intuition and reasoning,
   we are led to believe
that humans came to know good and evil
   in their increasing awareness of choice
     between selfish and unselfish behaviour,
   during many generations
     of evolving moral self-awareness
       and developing social values.

Was it your children's yearning for perfection
   that led to their belief
     that once upon a time mankind had been perfect,
       from which state they had fallen?

As they discovered more and more about you,
   in step with your revelation of yourself,
     mankind increasingly perceived
       not only the need for laws,
         but also the centrality of love.

They sought forgiveness, and hoped for eternal life,
   and longed for the Messiah.

Both they and we found our anointed king,
   perfect in every way,
     in the life of Jesus.

In his death and resurrection was seen mankind in perfection,
   at one with you yourself,
ensuring our own at-one-ness,
   in boundless divine eternity.

The Second Sunday of Lent

Genesis 12:1–4a; Psalm 121; Romans 4:1–5, 13–17; John 3:1–17.

Lord of our life,
  and God of our salvation,

Abraham trusted in you
  when you directed him
    from his own country
      to a new land,
    with the promise of becoming
      a great nation.

You are the guardian of Israel
  as the generations come and go,
    and will be for evermore,
      for you neither slumber nor sleep.

Abraham's faith in you
  counted for righteousness,
    and his reward was not a wage,
      paid as his due,
        for good work accomplished,
      but was the free and generous gift
      of your Spirit.

Nicodemus knew Jesus was sent from you,
  and as he sought to find your kingdom,
  he faced up to the call and condition
    to be born again
      from water and Spirit.

It was not to judge the world
  that you sent your Son into the world,
    but out of love for all mankind,
that through him,
  by death and resurrection,
    the world might not perish
      but be saved by faith,
        and enter eternal life.

The Third Sunday of Lent

Exodus 17:1–7; Psalm 95; Romans 5:1–11; John 4:5–42.

Lord of the living water,
    the purest of springs within us,
        welling up from the deep,
           and bringing eternal life,

'Give us water to drink, lest we die of thirst'
    was the cry made by Moses,
from a people whose hearts had gone astray
    in a wilderness of their own making,
        discerning not the ways of their God.

The same cry, spoken or unspoken,
    goes out today from lost and thirsty souls,
        and still you are put to the test
           with the question –
           'Is the Lord in our midst or not?'

But now we know that Messiah has come,
    whose meat and drink it is to do your will,
        until he has finished his work.

We follow his bidding
    and look around at the fields
        of human endeavour,
        and spiritual seeking,
           already ripe for harvest.

We rejoice in the divine glory
    that is to be ours,
        and we accept present suffering
           as a source of endurance,
               and approval of hope,
                  a hope that is no fantasy.

Be with those who need the strength of your grace,
    grant patience to those troubled in their anxieties,
        and in the peace of knowledge of forgiveness
           lift their hearts in joy and thanksgiving.

The Fourth Sunday of Lent

1 Samuel 16:1–13; Psalm 23; Ephesians 5:8–14; John 9:1–41.

Lord of light,
   healer of the blind,
      even of the blind from birth,
         who have never seen
            the glories of creation,

You are our shepherd and guide
   when we walk through valleys
      of deepest darkness,
and we fear no harm
   for you are there with us,
      your staff and crook giving us comfort.

Help us, as pilgrims, to be a light to others,
   untroubled by the shallow arguments
      of those who try to deceive,
   and taking neither part nor pleasure
      in barren deeds of darkness.

Give us wisdom, courage and strength
   to learn to judge for ourselves
      what is pleasing to you,
proving ourselves as children of the light,
   where there is a harvest
      of goodness, righteousness and truth.

When called upon to speak the truth before God,
   may we be able to say
      'I was blind and now I see,'
and in response to the question
   'Have you faith in the Son of Man?'
      may we respond with conviction,
         'Lord, I believe.'

Mothering Sunday

Years A, B, and C.

Exodus 2:1–10 (*or* 1 Samuel 1:20–28); Psalm 34:11–20 (*or* Psalm 127:1–4); 2 Corinthians 1:3–7 (*or* Colossians 3:12–17); Luke 2:33–35 (*or* John 19:25–27).

Lord of the love
  that binds everything together
    and completes the whole,

let the love of father and mother,
  each for the other,
    engender the love of both for their children,
    and fill the family with joy.

Show your compassion
  to those who endeavour to conceive
    and yet remain childless.
May their consolation be
  the sharing of disappointment and suffering,
    not only with others that are childless,
but with those who suffer as parents
  because of their children,
    as did Mary the mother of Jesus.

You, Lord, are close to those whose courage is broken,
  and you rescue those whose spirit is crushed,
    bringing consolation and strength
      to face with fortitude the unfairness of chance.

Our hope is firmly grounded
  if we clothe ourselves with compassion and kindness,
    humility, gentleness and patience,
      and are tolerant with each other and forever forgiving.

Let all our words and actions be in the name of Jesus,
  with the giving of thanks, through him,
    to you, our heavenly Father.

The Fifth Sunday of Lent

Passiontide begins.

Ezekiel 37:1−14; Psalm 130; Romans 8:6−11; John 11:1−45.

Lord of life,
    when faced with the death of a friend,
        you wept with those who were weeping
           in their deep distress.

Grant us the faith
    that sees death as the sleep
        awaiting the resurrection,
no longer doubting, like Thomas,
    your power to wake our souls,
        and lead us to believe.

By your love unfailing
    hear our cry,
for our souls wait for you
    more eagerly than watchmen
        awaiting the morning,
since you alone can set us free
    from all our sins.

Gather together the dried-out bones
    of our complacency,
and rattle them into conjunction
    with the sinews of a lively faith,
so that the Spirit of life and peace
    may breathe into us
        and enable us to stand
           before your face.

Possess us with the Spirit of Christ,
    so that we belong to the risen Christ
        and receive new life
           in our mortal bodies.

Palm Sunday

Years A, B and C. The Liturgy of the Palms.

Psalm 118:1–2, 19–29 (*or* Psalm 118:19–24); *Year A:* Matthew 21:1–11; *Year B:* Mark 11:1–11; (*or* John 12:12–16); *Year C:* Luke 19:28–40.

Lord of the way,
  you rode a donkey's foal on the way to Jerusalem.

The crowds that knew you
  spread their cloaks
    on the donkey,
    on the road,
  cut branches from the trees,
    palms in abundance,
  and shouted in greeting
    'Hosanna to the Son of David!'
    'Lord, preserve this Son of David!'

The whole city was in turmoil, wild with excitement,
  yet there were those who needed to ask
    'Who is this?'
and it was sufficient to answer
  'The prophet Jesus from Nazareth,'
    for, in truth, the whole could not be told.

It is good to give thanks to you Lord,
  for your steadfast love endures for ever.

The gates of victory and righteousness
  are opened up at your approach,
    for you have become our deliverer.

You were rejected like a stone discarded by builders,
  but by the grace of God, you were fashioned to become
    the chief corner-stone, the rock of our rejoicing.

'This is the day which the Lord has made,
  let us rejoice and be glad in it.'

Palm Sunday

Years A, B and C. The Liturgy of the Passion.

Isaiah 50:4–9a; Psalm 31:9–16 (*or* Psalm 31:9–18); Philippians 2:5–11;
Year A: Matthew 26:14–27: 66 (*or* Matthew 27:11–54); *Year B:* Mark
14:1–15: 47 (*or* Mark 15:1–39 [40–47]); *Year C:* Luke 22:14–23: 56 (*or*
Luke 23:1–49).

Lord our God, Son of God,
  Son of Man, Messiah,

you shared our human lot, and humbled yourself,
  hiding not your face from insult and spitting,
    obedient to the point of death.

Of your disciples,
  willing in spirit, but weak in flesh,
one betrayed you,
  another three times disowned you, and the rest ran away.

Support us by your Spirit in our renewed resolve
  never to betray you
    by failing to think through our beliefs,
    or by bowing to outside pressures,
  never to disown you
    by failing to witness,
    or by neglecting to pray,
  and never to run away
    by abandoning your teaching,
    or by breaking your commandments.

In the breaking of bread
  let us remember the breaking of your body;
in the blessing of wine
  let us remember the blood of the new covenant;
and in your resurrection
  let us recognize the fulfilment of your incarnation,
      and lift up our hearts and minds
          in thanks and praise.

Monday of Holy Week

Years A, B and C.

Isaiah 42:1–9; Psalm 36:5–11; Hebrews 9:11–15; John 12:1–11.

Lord of the sanctuary,
  entered once for all
  to secure for every people
    an eternal liberation,

You do not shout or raise your voice in the streets,
a bruised reed is safe in your hands,
you do not snuff out a smouldering wick,
and you never falter
  while coasts and islands await your teaching.

Earlier prophecies have come to pass,
  and now you declare new things,
with liberation from sins of the old covenant,
    consciences cleansed from the deadness of former ways,
      and promised entry into the eternal inheritance.

Frail mortals are filled
  with rich plenty in your house,
and you give them to drink
  from the stream of your delights,
    for you are the fountain of life,
and continue your saving power towards the honest of heart.

In the midst of a meal
  with your friend once dead,
    but then restored to life,
your feet that trod the way of peace
  were anointed with costly perfume,
    its fragrance filling the house;
and by this gracious act in life
  was foreshadowed the day of your burial,
    in itself a preparation
      for your resurrection glory.

Tuesday of Holy Week

Years A, B and C.

Isaiah 49:1–7; Psalm 71:1–14 (*or* Psalm 71:1–8); 1 Corinthians 1:18–31;
John 12:20–36.

Lord of power and glory,
  raised above the rabble
    of blind prejudice and hate,
  drawing all people to yourself,

The message of your cross,
  counted folly by the worldly,
    is wiser than human wisdom,
  and counted as weakness by the world,
    is stronger than human strength.

What was foolishness
  to those on the way to destruction
    has become the power of God
      to those on the way to salvation.

In you, Lord, we have our liberation
  into wisdom and heartfelt peace,
  through service and care for others,
  as we wait with steadfast hope.

When your soul was troubled,
  as the testing hour approached,
you faced the demands of glory
  and sought no way of escape.

Now those who say 'We would like to see Jesus'
  see you lifted up from the earth,
    a light in darkness, shining in glory,
      so that they, and we, may become children of light.

Open our eyes to see your perfection,
  open our ears to hear your message
    in answer to our prayer.

Wednesday of Holy Week

Years A, B and C.

Isaiah 50:4−9a; Psalm 70; Hebrews 12:1−3; John 13:21−32.

Lord of all joy,
   both here and in the world to come,

the joy set before you
   enabled you to endure the cross,
     ignoring its disgrace,
   and led to your seat in heaven.

You are the pioneer and perfecter of our faith,
   on whom we fix our eyes
     to run with resolution
       the race that is set before us,
         throwing off every encumbrance.

Help us to think of you
   when the going is rough,
that we grow not weary,
   nor begin to lose heart.

You discerned the weaknesses of your disciples,
   yet you did not intervene,
     except to give warning to Peter,
     and to tell Judas to hurry,
and they, in their confidence,
   thought they understood
     and did not listen,
and the other disciples failed to comprehend.

Grant that we may discern our weaknesses,
   listen to what you have to say to us,
   and endeavour to understand,
     to be obedient,
     and to go out into the night
       confident that you are with us.

Maundy Thursday

Years A, B and C.

Exodus 12:1–4, [5–10,] 11–14; Psalm 116:1–2, 12–19 (*or* Psalm 116:11–
19); 1 Corinthians 11:23–26; John 13:1–17, 31b–35.

Lord of the Passover,

> when you see the blood of sacrifice
> > on the doorposts and lintel of our hearts,
> pass over us,
> > sparing our life.

In memory of the sealing of the new covenant
> by the blood of Jesus,
we take bread, give thanks, break it and eat,
and take the cup and drink,
> proclaiming the death of our Lord,
> and handing on the tradition
> > which came from you yourself.

You have set us an example as Teacher and Lord,
> by the washing of feet.
Your washing is sufficient to make us entirely clean,
> so that we share with you
> > the love that has no end.

Constrain us to follow you,
> to wash one another's feet,
> > and to wipe with a towel,
> > > like a well-trained servant,
knowing that we are not greater than our Master,
> nor as messengers are we greater than the one who sends us.

Let your new commandment,
> to love one another, as you have loved us,
> > become the hallmark of our faith,
so that by this everyone will know
> that we are your disciples.

Good Friday

Years A, B and C.

Isaiah 52:13 – 53:12; Psalm 22:1–31 (*or* Psalm 22:1–11, *or* 1–21);
Hebrews 10:16–25 (*or* Hebrews 4:14–16; 5:7–9); John 18:1 – 19:42.

Lord of mercy,
  Lord of compassion,

you were shown neither mercy nor compassion,
  when you were condemned,
    and tortured, and killed.

Your willingness to suffer until death
  makes us aware of your presence when we suffer,
    and when we face death.

Give us grace to learn in the school of suffering,
  especially when that suffering appears to be undeserved.

When we confess that we deserve to suffer
  as a result of our offences,
help us to experience the joy and peace of your forgiveness,
and to see that your measure of suffering
  was, and is, and ever will be
    great enough to cancel all the suffering
      that would have been our due.

Be with those who suffer in innocence,
  those being tortured,
  those in danger of violence,
  the prisoners of conscience,
  those rejected as of no value.

In the wisdom of your compassion,
  let their outstretched hands be touched by yours,
so that they may know with you
  that your work of reconciliation
  is fully accomplished.

Easter Eve

Years A, B and C. In RCL this is Holy Saturday.

These readings are for use at services other than the Easter Vigil.

Job 14:1−14 (*or* Lamentations 3:1−9, 19−24); Psalm 31:1−4, 15−16 (*or* Psalm 31:1−5); 1 Peter 4:1−8; Matthew 27:57−66 (*or* John 19:38−42).

Lord in waiting,
  grant us patience to wait,
    and to expand our hope.

Help us to taste death with you,
  by crucifying our evil desires,
  and by being cradled
    in the tomb of our rebirth.

Enrich our trust,
  and purify our beliefs,
    so that we may survive
      the thrusting spears
        of doubt and inner conflict.

Bathe the wounds in our self-identity
  with the balm of your blessing,

and wrap us in the clean linen sheet
  of forgiveness and promise,
    perfumed with spices,
      the myrrh of mortality
      and the sweet-smelling aloes
      of other-worldliness,

so that in the absence,
  and in the silence,
    our hearts may grow fonder,
    and find their rest in you.

Easter Vigil

Years A, B and C.

Exodus 14:10–31; 15:20–21; plus two alternative Old Testament readings;
Psalm 114; Romans 6:3–11;
Year A: Matthew 28:1–10; *Year B:* Mark 16:1–8; *Year C:* Luke 24:1–12.

Lord of liberation,
　　delivering Israel from the Egyptians,
　　raising Jesus from the dead,
　　　　with whom we are united in his resurrection,

Open our minds to comprehend
　　what it meant to the Israelites
　　　　to be in terror of Pharaoh,
　　　　　　and clamouring to you for help.
They were aware of the angel that led them,
　　as he moved to the rear to protect them,
　　　　and they walked to their salvation
　　　　　　on what was to them dry ground,
　　　　responding with awe,
　　　　　　and renewing their faith in you.

When your people needed water,
　　you turned the rock into a pool,
　　　　and the flinty cliff into a welling spring.

In the waters of baptism we are united with Jesus,
　　immersed in his death,
　　　　identified with him in resurrection,
　　　　　　setting out on a new life.

At the empty tomb, the angel told the two Marys,
　　'You have nothing to fear,' and, trusting this assurance,
　　　　they hurried away in awe and great joy.

Grant that when we, like the two Marys, meet Jesus on the road,
　　we may kneel before him, and be told by him,
　　　　'Do not be afraid.'

Easter Day

Acts 10:34−43 (*or* Jeremiah 31:1−6); Psalm 118:1−2, 14−24 (*or* Psalm 118:14−24). Colossians 3:1−4 (*or* Acts 10:34−43); John 20:1−18 (*or* Matthew 28:1−10).

Lord of all life and power,
   the stone the builders rejected,
      which has now become the main corner-stone,

we are raised with you
   to seek the things that are above.

Like your disciples,
   when they realised you were risen,
      we are freed from fear,
and like the women,
   when they found the stone rolled away
      from the tomb of their sadness,
         and heard your voice,
            we stand in awe.

Stir our hearts and minds
   to declare and sing our thanksgiving
      for your transformation
         from the dead to the living,
so that others may hear and believe
   how in every nation
      those who are God-fearing,
         and do what is right,
            are acceptable to God.

Let us with great joy
   draw water from the wells of salvation,
      and cease to dwell on days gone by,
but rather comprehend the new thing
   that breaks from the bud
      of the tree of life.

Grant that we, with all your people of every nation,
      may keep this Easter feast
         with the unleavened bread of sincerity, and truth.

Easter Evening

RCL: Years A, B and C.

Isaiah 25:6–9; Psalm 114; 1 Corinthians 5:6b–8; Luke 24:13–49.

Lord of the new leaven,
   the little that leavens the whole,
help us to get rid of the old leaven of malice and evil
   to become the new unleavened dough of sincerity and truth.

Grant us special grace to understand the Scriptures,
   destroying the veil that shrouded the prophets,
     the pall thrown over all the nations,
so that we may say, 'This is the Lord for whom we have waited'
   and share in the feasting, with rich fare
     and well-matured wines, strained clear.

How dull we are, as dull as any disciples,
   how slow to understand what the prophets said.
And though our hearts may at times be on fire,
   how slow we are to recognize your presence.

We too talk together and argue about all that happened in Jerusalem.
We rehearse the familiar reports of astonishment and disbelief,
   and wonder how the warnings of Jesus
     concerning the Messiah and his sufferings
       could have been forgotten or misunderstood.

The two that walked to Emmaus listened to Jesus
   as he explained to them the Scriptures concerning himself,
but their eyes were not opened until the breaking of bread,
   recognizing Jesus before he quickly vanished.
They hastened to Jerusalem to share the news,
   and Jesus joined them – to find them startled and terrified,
     thinking him to be a ghost.
Even after showing hands and feet and inviting them to touch him,
   doubts arose in their minds, still incredulous and astounded –
     it seemed to be a truth too hard to believe.

Lord, we believe. Help our unbelief.

The Second Sunday of Easter

Acts 2:14a, 22–32; Psalm 16; 1 Peter 1:3–9; John 20:19–31. *For those who require an Old Testament reading: Exodus 14:10–31; 15:20–21, to be read before the reading from Acts.*

Lord of living evidence,
  in your hands and feet and side,
    sufficient to convince
      both those who saw
      and those who heard their report,
        but did not see,

David was confident
  from wisdom imparted at night to his inmost being,
  that Messiah would not experience corruption.

He was shown the path of life,
  and found fullness of joy in your presence.

You gave us new birth into a living hope,
an inheritance that nothing can destroy,
  or spoil or wither,
    because of our faith in you,
faith which stands the test,
  and is more precious than perishable gold.

Our trust in Jesus,
  the gift of your Spirit,
  fills us with joy too great for words,
    as we reap faith's harvest,
      salvation for our souls.

Open the inner eyes of those who say,
  'Unless I can see, and touch,
    I will never believe,'
so that they are touched in their hearts
  and feel bound to say,
    'My Lord and my God,'
  and know the power of your greeting,
    'Peace be with you.'

The Third Sunday of Easter

Acts 2:14a, 36–41; Psalm 116:1–4, 12–19 (*or* Psalm 116:1–8); 1 Peter 1:17–23; Luke 24:13–35. *For those who require an Old Testament reading: Zephaniah 3:14–20, to be read before the reading from Acts.*

Lord of the obvious,
   when seen with hindsight,

how often are we like your disciples
   on the road to Emmaus,
hoping that Jesus was the liberator of Israel,
   yet failing to look and perceive,
   failing to recognize your way of speaking,
      and needing your revelation
         in the breaking of bread?

How hard it is for us to understand
   their lack of attention,
   their obtuse despair,
   and their disbelief in the reports of others,
until we realise
   that these are our own failings.

You gave your disciples freedom
   from the futility of traditional ways of thought,
      inherited from their ancestors.

Set our hearts on fire
   and enlighten our thoughts,
      to see the glory
         of the risen Christ.

Purify our souls
   through obedience to your truth,
so that we feel sincere affection towards fellow Christians,
   and love one another whole-heartedly
      with all our strength,
knowing we are born again of immortal parentage,
   through the imperishable seed
      of the living and enduring
         word of God.

The Fourth Sunday of Easter

Acts 2:42–47; Psalm 23; 1 Peter 2:19–25; John 10:1–10. *For those who require an Old Testament reading: Genesis 7, to be read before the reading from Acts.*

Shepherd and guardian of our souls,
   leading your sheep,
   tending your lambs,
   guarding them from danger,
   calling them by name,

bring us to green pastures,
   where there is water
      to quench our thirst,
         and revive our spirits.

When we walk through valleys
   in deepest gloom,
comfort us with your staff,
reassure us with your shepherd's crook,
   so that we fear no evil.

Bind us together in the fullness of life
   so that we do not stray,
   or drift away from your sight
      and fall prey
         to the wolves of this world.

Grant that we may see you ever before us
   as our example
      in suffering for others,
      in attending to their needs,
      in sharing a common life,
      in prayer and the breaking of bread,
   knowing the way,
   drawing us forward,

until we reach safety in the fold
   of eternal salvation,
      with you as the door.

The Fifth Sunday of Easter

Acts 7:55–60; Psalm 31:1–5, 15–16 (*or* Psalm 31:1–5); 1 Peter 2:2–10; John 14:1–14. *For those who require an Old Testament reading: Genesis 8:1–19, to be read before the reading from Acts.*

Lord of rocks and stones,
   our rock of refuge and our stronghold,
   our living stone,
     rejected by mankind,
      chosen by God,
   the main corner-stone,
     yet a stone to trip over,
     and a rock to stumble against,

Stephen by his witness was rewarded,
   by a vision of the Son of Man,
     standing at the right hand of God,
   and by a volley of stones,
     from a lynching mob, approved by Saul,
praying, as he died,
   'Lord, do not hold this sin against them.'

You set us free from the net
   that is hidden to catch us,
and care for us in our distress,
   granting us untrammelled liberty.

Fashion us, we pray, as living stones
   to be built into a spiritual temple,
   to form a holy and royal priesthood
     to offer spiritual sacrifice,
      as a dedicated nation.

The source of the words you spoke
   was the indwelling Father,
and knowing you, we know the Father.

You are the way, the truth, and the life,
   in whom we trust
     for whatever we ask
      in your name.

The Sixth Sunday of Easter

Acts 17:22–31; Psalm 66:8–20; 1 Peter 3:13–22; John 14:15–21. *For those who require an Old Testament reading: Genesis 8:20 – 9:17, to be read before the reading from Acts.*

Lord of those who seek,
    groping after you,
        in the hope of finding you,
            hitherto their Unknown God,

Grant that the 'Men of Athens' of this age
    may likewise be uncommonly scrupulous
        in everything that concerns religion.

When they search for you
    in shrines made by human hands,
may they find you living in their hearts,
    the universal giver of life.

Let us not be intimidated
    when we are eager to do what is good,
nor fear when challenged to defend,
    with courtesy and respect,
        the hope that is in us.

In our baptism
    we appealed to you
        for a good conscience,
and found our salvation
    into resurrection life.

If we love you,
    we shall obey your commands,
and our indwelling advocate,
    the Spirit of Truth,
        will be with us for ever.

Ascension Day

Years A, B and C.

Acts 1:1–11 (*or* Daniel 7:9–14); Psalm 47 (*or* Psalm 93); Ephesians 1:15–23 (*or* Acts 1:1–11); Luke 24:44–53. *The reading from Acts must be used as either the first or second reading.*

Lord of the ascension of mankind,
   in you, and through you, to God the Father,

We see you, in Trinity, as filling the universe
   with the fullness of your authority, throughout all ages;
in past ages,
   when your people clapped their hands,
     rejoicing in your awesome reign over all nations,
in this present age,
   in the glories revealed by science,
and in the age to come,
   in glories beyond imagination.

Your kingly power which can never be destroyed,
   is mightier than the breakers of the sea,
     rolling in majesty to wash the shores of distant nations.

In the act of blessing, you parted from your disciples,
   with a cloud to hide you from their sight.

In the act of blessing,
   unite us with the promised gift of the Holy Spirit,
   and lift the cloud that veils our inward eyes
     from the revelation of your loving mercy,
that we may know the hope of the resources of power
   given to those who trust in you.

May we ascend in spirit
   by discarding the burdens of sin,
     and receiving the grace of forgiveness.

The Seventh Sunday of Easter

The Sunday after Ascension Day.

Acts 1:6–14; Psalm 68:1–10, 32–35 (*or* Psalm 68:1–10); 1 Peter 4:12–14;
5:6–11; John 17:1–11. *For those who require an Old Testament reading:*
Ezekiel 36:24–28, to be read before the reading from Acts.

Lord God,
   the only true God,
in your care for us, you invite us
   to cast all our anxiety upon you.

When we are mocked and despised
   for being Christians,
help us to count ourselves happy
   to share in the sufferings of Christ
     with our fellow Christians.

Let those who are hostile and stubborn
   be melted in their hearts
     like wax near the fire.

For those who rebel or default,
   and endure the scorching desert
     of self-imposed despair,
       being blind to your purpose
        and unfathomable love,
   grant that they may finally receive
     a new heart, and a new spirit,
     by a new vision of your grace.

Holy God,
   protect us by the power of your name,
that we may be one,
   in and between ourselves,
     as you are one,
and be your people,
   with you as our only God.

The Day of Pentecost

Whit Sunday.

Acts 2:1–21 (*or* Numbers 11:24–30); Psalm 104:24–34, 35b (*or* Psalm 104:24–35); 1 Corinthians 12:3b–13 (*or* Acts 2:1–21); John 20:19–23 (*or* John 7:37–39). *The reading from Acts must be used as either the first or second reading.*

Holy Spirit, Lord of grace and power,
   help us to recognize, and see the beneficial purpose,
      of the particular varieties of gifts
         that you bestow on each one of us.

Encourage young men and women
   with the gift of imagination,
      that they may see those visions which they can strive to fulfil,
let the older men and women
   dream the dreams of the just,
      remembering the spirit of their youth,
and let our sons and daughters
   prophesy in your name,
      understand with their wits,
         and declare your continuing revelation.

Breathe on us the breath of life,
   the oxygen of our souls,
      feeding the spiritual fire of our existence.

Let streams of living water flow within us,
   cleansing and feeding, and communicating purity.

Direct the aerials of our minds
   to receive the wealth of information
      in the heaven-sent messages you transmit
         for our daily reception,
and let us tune ourselves
   to resonate with your will,
      declare 'Jesus is Lord,'
         and receive your peace.

Trinity Sunday

Isaiah 40:12–17, 27–31; Psalm 8; 2 Corinthians 13:11–13; Matthew 28:16–20.

Lord God in eternity,
   Triune in Trinity,
      thrice Holy in Divinity,
expand our vision of your greatness,
   for we know in our contingency
      and in the depths of our dependence,
         how much we are less than you.

Even though we are being made in your image,
   you are the Lord of the order of nature,
      and we can never be master over all that you have made.

We are frail in our mortality,
   and though we measure the waters of the sea,
      and weigh mountains,
we could never stand at your side
   to counsel and instruct the Spirit of truth.

Win for us new strength in declaring your love,
   that we may soar as on eagles' wings,
      run and not feel faint,
         march on boldly and not grow weary.

Your disciples knelt in worship of Jesus,
   though some were doubtful,
      and so, in truth, it is today.

Help us to teach others by our example,
   observing all that you have commanded us to do,
      mending our ways to agree with one another,
         and living in peace.

With the wisdom and insight that you have lavished on us all,
   enable us to discern your secret purpose,
that everything in the universe
   is to be brought into unity with the love of Christ,
      our Saviour, Lord and God.

A Day of Thanksgiving for Holy Communion

Years A, B and C. The Thursday after Trinity Sunday (Corpus Christi).

Genesis 14:18–20; Psalm 116:12–19; 1 Corinthians 11:23–26; John 6:51–58.

Lord Most High,
  Lord of flesh and blood
    in your incarnation,
  Lord of bread and wine
    in Holy Communion,

We break the bread, and eat it,
bless the cup, and drink it,
and do this in memory of you,
  proclaiming your death until you come again.

You are the living bread,
  come down from heaven,
    given for the life of the world.

We lift up the cup of salvation,
  the cup of blessing,
    a thank-offering,
  the new covenant
    sealed by your blood.

By the bread and wine of Communion,
  real food and real drink,
    we have eternal life,
      and dwell in you
      as you dwell in us.

This is our sacrifice of praise and thanksgiving,
in which we are renewed by your Spirit,
  inspired by your love,
  united in your body, the Church,
    and so united with you.

Proper 4

The Sunday between 29 May and 4 June inclusive (if after Trinity Sunday).

Continuous: Genesis 6:9–22; 7:24; 8:14–19; Psalm 46; *or Related:* Deuteronomy 11:18–21, 26–28; Psalm 31:1–5, 19–24 (*or* Psalm 31:19–24). Romans 1:16–17; 3:22b–28, [29–31]; Matthew 7:21–29.

Lord, Lord,
grant us freely of your grace,
for we can never earn it,
nor deserve it.

Even if we keep your law,
prophesy in your name,
cast out demons,
and perform many miracles,
our deeds can be evil,
if they are lacking in love.

Help us to perceive and welcome
the will of our heavenly Father,
upholding the law,
but not being bound by its letter,
when its spirit is in question.

Guide us, not only to read your words,
and to mark, learn and inwardly digest them,
but to hear your voice,
and in stillness and silence to listen to your call.

Deepen our faith,
our trust, our belief, and our hope,
and teach us to know that you are God,
our refuge and our stronghold,
a timely help in trouble.

Proper 5

The Sunday between 5 and 11 June inclusive (if after Trinity Sunday).

Continuous: Genesis 12:1–9; Psalm 33:1–12; *or Related:* Hosea 5:15 – 6:6;
Psalm 50:7–15;
Romans 4:13–25; Matthew 9:9–13, 18–26.

God of Abraham,
　　author of his faith,
we see that faith as the ground of your promise to him,
　　and see his belief as given by grace alone.

You were the leader of your people,
　　even when their loyalty was like the morning mist,
　　and like dew that vanishes early.

Some of your children,
　　in their remorse,
　　　　returned to you,
　　and in their distress,
　　　　they searched diligently for you,
　　　　　　and strove to know their Lord.

Reveal to us, as you revealed to them,
　　the importance of loyalty beyond reproach,
　　　　and of the granting of mercy above sacrifice,
　　　　and of acknowledgement of your unfailing love
　　　　　　above whole offerings.

It is not the healthy who need a doctor
　　but the sick.
You did not come to call the virtuous
　　but the sinners.

Grant us the grace to hear your call,
　　to discern your message,
　　　　to know the power of your healing touch,
　　　　　　the life in the grasp of your hand,
　　　　　　　　the quality of wholeness.

Proper 6

The Sunday between 12 and 18 June inclusive (if after Trinity Sunday).

Continuous: Genesis 18:1–15, [21:1–7]; Psalm 116:1–2, 12–19 (*or* Psalm 116:11–18); *or Related:* Exodus 19:2–8a; Psalm 100; Romans 5:1–8; Matthew 9:35 – 10:8, [9–23].

Lord of the harvest of souls,
  a heavy crop,
    but the labourers too few,

Show us what is needed in this age,
  to draw men and women to you,
    that they may believe your message.

Prepare us to receive the authority
  to speak and to act;
    the same authority that you gave to your disciples.

Inspire us to understand
  why so many find it hard to believe,
    especially good people,
      caring for others,
        honest in their seeking.

Is it because we do not dwell entirely in you?
Or must we admit that your words
  do not meaningfully dwell in us,
    and so lack meaning for others?

We so often fall short,
  in our steadfast endeavours,
    diligently to heed and to keep
      your commands.

Grant us forgiving grace
  to ask with confidence in your name,
    believing that such requests
      will never go unanswered.

Proper 7

The Sunday between 19 and 25 June inclusive (if after Trinity Sunday).

Continuous: Genesis 21:8–21; Psalm 86:1–10, 16–17 (*or* Psalm 86:1–10); *or Related:* Jeremiah 20:7–13; Psalm 69:7–10, [11–15,] 16–18 (*or* Psalm 69:13–18);
Romans 6:1b–11; Matthew 10:24–39.

Lord of the world of mankind,
   you knew, and know,
      the reproach of fellow humans.

Like the Psalmist and Jeremiah,
   many of us too have been ridiculed for our beliefs,
and some of us have found enemies
   even under our own roof.

Lord of all, hear our prayer,
   and grant us an answer
      to the temptation
         to hide our beliefs.

Let us not think to say
   'I shall not speak in his name again,'
      lest your word becomes imprisoned within us,
         like a fire burning in our hearts.

You did not come to bring peace to the earth,
   the false peace of pride and indifference,
      with self-seeking pleasure,
nor did you fear those who can kill the body,
   but cannot kill the soul.

You brought true peace,
   of heart and mind and soul,
especially to those who in the fullness of trust and hope
   put the search for truth above even life in an earthly body,
and by so doing win through to eternal life.

Proper 8

The Sunday between 26 June and 2 July inclusive.

Continuous: Genesis 22:1−14; Psalm 13; *or Related:* Jeremiah 28:5−9; Psalm 89:1−4, 15−18 (*or* Psalm 89:8−18);
Romans 6:12−23; Matthew 10:40−42.

Lord of all creation,
    author of the play of life,
        you draw us out in the drama of sacrifice.

Abraham did not argue,
    when asked to kill his son;
Isaac did not struggle
    when bound for the fire.

Their trust was grounded
    in the ritual of their time,
    and in the force of your commands.

But you taught them abhorrence
    for such human sacrifice,
and, as the saying goes,
    'In the mountain of the Lord
        it was provided.'

Help us to yield whole-hearted obedience
    to your pattern of teaching,
        to which you made us subject.

Replace our yielding to the temptations of moral anarchy,
    and the dangers of outdated tradition,
with zeal to follow your word,
    and wait for what you provide
        'in the mountain of the Lord'.

May we also provide, for your children,
    cups of cold, refreshing water,
and welcome the prophets of our time
    and the saints of our age.

Proper 9

The Sunday between 3 and 9 July inclusive.

Continuous: Genesis 24:34−38, 42−49, 58−67; Psalm 45:10−17; *or Related:*
Zechariah 9:9−12; Psalm 145:8−14;
Romans 7:15−25a; Matthew 11:16−19, 25−30.

God of beauty, love and goodness,

we thank you for human love,
  uniting bodies, minds and souls
    with desire for beauty,
      and a sharing of joy.

You open your hand
  and satisfy every living creature
    with the favour of your grace and compassion,
    your long-suffering and faithfulness,
      a challenge and example for us to follow.

In our inmost selves we delight in your commandments,
and in our minds we will to do good,
  even when we do what we detest,
    held captive by our lower nature.

Help those who find themselves weary
  of the heavy burden of their lives,
who seek for the rest that only you can give.

Especially we pray for those
  with the heavy burdens of learning and wisdom
    who seek your easy yoke
      in the simplicity of childlike trust,
and yearn for a lighter load,
  with gentle and humble hearts,
    as they face the complexity of beliefs.

Who is there to rescue them?
  None but you alone,
    through Jesus Christ our Lord.

Proper 10

The Sunday between 10 and 16 July inclusive.

Continuous: Genesis 25:19–34; Psalm 119:105–112; *or Related:* Isaiah
55:10–13; Psalm 65:[1–8,] 9–13 (*or* Psalm 65:9–13);
Romans 8:1–11; Matthew 13:1–9, 18–23.

Lord of the word,
   sown like seed,
      in every variety of soil,
         in all the nations,

Help us to prepare the soil of our minds
   to produce a good crop of understanding,
that the fields of our experience
   may be wreathed in good pleasure,
and our families and friends,
   like the trees in the countryside,
      may clap their hands with delight.

Let not worldly cares
   and the false glamour of worldly possessions
      choke the growth of our faith,
nor let those who accept your word with joy
   quickly lose their faith
      in times of trouble or distress.

Let the life-giving law of the power of your Spirit
      set us free from the human weakness
         which robbed the old law of its potency.

By your indwelling Spirit
   help us to control our unspiritual nature,
that the abundance of the harvest
   produced by your gift of new life
      may be pleasing to you,
         through Jesus Christ our Lord.

Proper 11

The Sunday between 17 and 23 July inclusive.

Continuous: Genesis 28:10–19a; Psalm 139:1–12, 23–24 (*or* Psalm 139:1–12); *or Related:* Wisdom of Solomon 12:13, 16–19; Psalm 86:11–17; Romans 8:12–25; Matthew 13:24–30, 36–43.

Abba, Father,

you are our Lord and God,
  compassionate and gracious,
    long-suffering, ever faithful, ever true,
      our help and our comfort.

There is no other God but you,
  all the world is your concern.

Master of all, source of justice,
  you are lenient to all,
  you judge in mercy,
  and rule us with great forbearance,

and you taught us as your children
  that he who is just must also be kind-hearted.

Grant us the Spirit of adoption,
  that we may be more aware
    of being your children
      with much to learn.

Give us ears to hear,
  wills to listen to,
  and minds to comprehend
    the message of immortality
      for the children of your kingdom,
that we may look forward eagerly,
  and with patience,
    to entering at the last into glorious liberty,
      in the presence of Christ our Lord.

Proper 12

The Sunday between 24 and 30 July inclusive.

Continuous: Genesis 29:15–28; Psalm 105:1–11, 45b (*or* Psalm 105:1–11)
or Psalm 128; *or Related:* 1 Kings 3:5–12; Psalm 119:129–136;
Romans 8:26–39; Matthew 13:31–33, 44–52.

Lord God,
    you search our inmost being,
        and your Spirit seeks to interpret
            our needs.

Help us to be learners
    in the kingdom of heaven,

educate us through your word,
    in the light of revelation,

and give us understanding
    even when we know so little.

Let us learn from the mustard seed,
    with its great potential for growth,
and let us ever seek to recover
    the buried treasures of our discoveries,
        and hold on to pearls of great value.

Teach us how to pray,
    giving thanks for your blessings,
        and seeking your presence in all we do.

May we learn from Solomon's dream
    to ask for a heart with skill to listen,
and for discernment
    in all our judgements.

Let nothing in all creation
    separate us from your love,
        in Jesus Christ our Lord.

Proper 13

The Sunday between 31 July and 6 August inclusive.

Continuous: Genesis 32:22−31; Psalm 17:1−7, 15 (*or* Psalm 17:1−7); *or*
Related: Isaiah 55:1−5; Psalm 145:8−9, 14−21 (*or* Psalm 145:14−21);
Romans 9:1−5; Matthew 14:13−21.

God of Israel,
   Lord of all the nations that call to you in sincerity,
keep before our eyes
   the memory of your revelation,
   and the discoveries of mankind,
      inspired by your Spirit throughout the ages.

Israel was the apple of your eye,
   and when they raised their eyes to you
      you gave them their food in due season.

Yet so many descendants of Israel rejected you,
   causing great grief, and unceasing sorrow,
      in the hearts of those who believed.

Help us to be sensitive
   to the beliefs and feelings
      of all your children,
         whatever their reaction to the gospel.

Feed the hunger of their souls
   by multiplying the food of life
      that you have blessed and given to us,
and make for us opportunities to give to others,
   that all may partake
      and be satisfied.
Gather up the remains,
   to show the superabundance
      of your grace
         to all who seek to follow you.

Proper 14

The Sunday between 7 and 13 August inclusive.

Continuous: Genesis 37:1–4, 12–28; Psalm 105:1–6, 16–22, 45b (*or* Psalm 105:1–10); *or Related:* 1 Kings 19:9–18; Psalm 85:8–13; Romans 10:5–15; Matthew 14:22–33.

Lord of our faith,
  we expect and ask so much of you,
    and so often you choose to respond
      not in the fierceness of wind,
      not in the rock-splitting earthquake,
      not in the consuming crackle of fire,
        but in the still, small voice.

Help us to distinguish your voice,
  even when it is a disturbing voice,
    from the confusing murmurings
      of our inward conversations,
        that seek comfort rather than courage.

When we worship you,
  we sense your presence is near,
and in your gift of deliverance from fear
  we see that love and faithfulness have come together,
    and justice and mercy have embraced.

Let the grace of this deliverance
  be sensed throughout our nation,
and send a Joseph of our time
  to correct the errors of the officers of this realm,
    and to teach the counsellors wisdom,
      to your honour and glory.

When we set out in faith
  to join you in the storms of life,
let us not hesitate,
  lest we begin to sink,
    and need a miracle to survive.

Proper 15

The Sunday between 14 and 20 August inclusive.

Continuous: Genesis 45:1–15; Psalm 133; *or Related:* Isaiah 56:1, 6–8;
Psalm 67;
Romans 11:1–2a, 29–32; Matthew 15:[10–20,] 21–28.

God of mercy
  whose purpose is liberation
for all those imprisoned
  by their wilful disobedience,

guide the nations of the earth
  to live together as brothers
    in the fulfilling strength of unity.

Be gracious to all
  and bless us,
that your purpose may be known to all,
  your saving power among the nations.

In your house of prayer for all nations,
  open our hearts to your love,
  open our ears to your word,
  and open our minds to give us understanding.

Let persistence in our faith
  be rewarded by wholesome scraps
    from our Master's table.

Deliver us from the famine of faith
  in this present generation,
and when we eat at your table
  purify our hearts,
    that they be not the source
      of words that defile us,
  and fill our mouths instead, by your grace,
    with praise and thanksgiving.

Proper 16

The Sunday between 21 and 27 August inclusive.

Continuous: Exodus 1:8 – 2:10; Psalm 124; *or Related:* Isaiah 51:1–6; Psalm 138; Romans 12:1–8; Matthew 16:13–20.

Lord Jesus,
> now we can, and do, declare
>> that you are Son of the living God,
>>> the Messiah,
and on this rock of faith in you, your Church is built.

Your love endures for ever,
> and you never abandon what you have made.

Your deliverance is everlasting,
> your saving power remains unbroken,
>> bringing gladness and joy
>>> in the garden of the Lord,
>>>> with thanksgiving and melody.

We offer our very selves to you
> with worship springing from mind and heart,
>> transformed by the renewal of our minds,
>>> perceiving the will of God.

Help us to form a sober estimate of ourselves,
> neither too high, nor too low,
>> and to recognize the gifts we have;

guide with inspiration those who speak,
> clothe with care those who administer,
> enrich with wisdom those who teach,
> increase the rapport of those who counsel,
> and draw towards you those who lead;

persuade those who can give to the needy
> to do so without grudging,
>> and warm the hearts of those
>>> who help their neighbours in distress;
for when we call, you answer us,
> and our help is in the name of the Lord.

Proper 17

The Sunday between 2 August and 3 September inclusive.

Continuous: Exodus 3:1−15; Psalm 105:1−6, 23−26, 45c (*or* Psalm 115); *or*
Related: Jeremiah 15:15−21; Psalm 26:1−8;
Romans 12:9−21; Matthew 16:21−28.

Lord God of Israel,
   you knew of the suffering of your children in Egypt,
      and delivered them from their oppressors.

Incarnate Lord,
   you knew you would suffer in Jerusalem,
      and deliver all mankind from the binding cords of sin.

Grant, as far as our nature allows,
   that we should think as you think
     of suffering and death,
     of the need to renounce self,
     of the rewards of the cross
       that you won in triumph,
      rewards that you give to those
        who take up their crosses and follow you.

Help us, by your Spirit, to love in all sincerity,
   with mutual affection for the Christian community,
   to let hope keep us joyful,
     persisting in prayer,
     practising hospitality,
   to rejoice with those who rejoice,
     and weep with those who weep,
   to let our aims be known to all and counted honourable,
     practised with unflagging zeal,
      aglow with the Spirit.

So far as is possible, grant us to live at peace with all,
   to be humble enough to enjoy the company of humble people,
   and never to be a stumbling-block
     of any kind, to any one.

Proper 18

Continuous: Exodus 12:1−14; Psalm 149; *or Related:* Ezekiel 33:7−11;
Psalm 119:33−40;
Romans 13:8−14; Matthew 18:15−20.

Lord God of Israel,
   how did you come to choose
     the Jews?

Was it because the need they felt to choose
   one God from among the many worshipped
     gave you the opportunity to guide them
       to accept your revelation?

Your love for all mankind,
   your neighbours in creation,
     was revealed through the prophets,
       and made explicit by Jesus.

After we choose to follow Jesus,
   we become increasingly aware
     that we too are chosen by you,
for the gift of the power of the Spirit is not earned by us,
   nor even deserved by our choice.

With the Psalmist we sing a new song,
   and rejoice in our Maker:
teach us, Lord, the way of your commands,
   to love our neighbour as ourselves;
dispose our hearts towards your instruction,
   not towards love of gain,
and turn our eyes away from all that is futile.

Clothe us with the armour of light,
   in the name of Jesus,
     so that where two or three are gathered together in his name,
       we may sense his presence and meet him among us.

Proper 19

The Sunday between 11 and 17 September inclusive.

Continuous: Exodus 14:19–31; Psalm 114 (*or Canticle*: Exodus 15:1b–11, 20–21); *or Related:* Genesis 50:15–21; Psalm 103:[1–7,] 8–13 (*or* Psalm 103:8–13);
Romans 14:1–12; Matthew 18:21–35.

Lord God of Israel,
   as the heavens are high above the earth,
      so outstanding is your love.

As a father has compassion on his children,
   so, Lord, you have compassion on us,
      and enable us to stand against
         enemies without,
            and within.

Grant that we may never look down
   on fellow Christians
      whom we consider to be weaker in the faith.

Help us to accept them,
   without debate about their misgivings,
      such as those concerning what they eat,
   or distinctions they observe
      between this day and that.

As we are all answerable to you,
   so everyone must act
      on his own convictions.

Give us compassion and grace
   to forgive our brothers
      more times than we can remember to count,
that thereby we may comfort them,
   and set their minds at rest,
      when they ask forgiveness,
         and it is granted in your name.

Proper 20

The Sunday between 18 and 24 September inclusive.

Continuous: Exodus 16:2–15; Psalm 105:1–6, 37–45 (*or* Psalm 105:37–45);
or Related: Jonah 3:10 – 4:11; Psalm 145:1–8;
Philippians 1:21–30; Matthew 20:1–16.

Lord God of the ages,
    Lord of the evolution of mankind,
        and of our beliefs about you,
            and about your creation,

In the histories of nations
    there are those who seek you
        with joy in their hearts,
    and there are mighty deeds and marvels,
        seen as the glorious splendour
            of your majesty.

As we meditate on your wonderful acts,
    we give you thanks,
        and vow to make known your power
            among all nations
                and among all peoples.

Your greatness is beyond all searching out,
    and when we are angry, even mortally angry,
        at our wounded pride
            when others give up their wicked ways
                and are forgiven,
        then we need your long-suffering
            and ever-constant compassion.

The wages of your service are fair.

Grant that we may never be jealous
    because you are generous,
for there is fruitful work for us to do
    in and through your name.

Proper 21

The Sunday between 25 September and 1 October inclusive.

Continuous: Exodus 17:1−7; Psalm 78:1−4, 12−16 (*or* Psalm 78:1−7); *or*
Related: Ezekiel 18:1−4, 25−32; Psalm 25:1−9;
Philippians 2:1−13; Matthew 21:23−32.

Lord, our God,
   to you we lift our hearts,
      in you we trust.

We remember your teaching,
   through the meaningful stories
      recounted through the generations,
   and the praiseworthy acts and wonders you have done.

Grant us grace
   not to grumble or complain when times are hard,
   nor to challenge your power,
      by questioning your presence among us.

Let us not impute the effects of our sins on our children,
   for you have made it abundantly clear,
      that it is the person who sins
         who will suffer,
      and each will be judged on his record.

Give us the grace
   to have a common attitude of mind,
      a common life in Christ,
         something to stir the heart
         with loving consolation and warmth of affection,
   and occasions to fill up cups of happiness,
      by looking to others' interests
         and not merely to our own.

Reassure us of the riches of resurrection life,
freed from any embarrassment
   from earthly relationships.

Proper 22

The Sunday between 2 and 8 October inclusive.

Continuous: Exodus 20:1–4, 7–9, 12–20; Psalm 19:1–14 (*or* Psalm 19:7–14); *or Related:* Isaiah 5:1–7; Psalm 80:7–15; Philippians 3:4b–14; Matthew 21:33–46.

Lord of the regularities and order of nature,
   sending out the daily sun,
     like a bridegroom from his bridal chamber,
      rejoicing to run his course,

One day speaks to another, day by day, and night by night,
   imparting knowledge without sound of any voice.

The sun shone on Israel, your vineyard,
   planted with the choice red wine of Judah,
   with its hedge and wall, watch-tower and wine vat,
     but it yielded a crop of wild grapes,
      cries of distress instead of righteousness.

Your servants, the prophets, were rejected by the labourers,
   and their message ignored.

You sent your only Son,
   with his unhurried pace,
     and self-revealing grace,
     and him they killed.

They believed not the scriptures,
   nor his very own word,
     that he would rise again,
     releasing the power of his resurrection.

Lord, let our one desire be to know Christ and his power,
   and to strive towards what lies ahead.

May the words we speak, and those we write,
   and the thoughts of our minds,
   be acceptable to you, Lord of our salvation.

Proper 23

The Sunday between 9 and 15 October inclusive.

Continuous: Exodus 32:1–14; Psalm 106:1–6, 19–23 (*or* Psalm 106:1–6);
or Related: Isaiah 25:1–9; Psalm 23;
Philippians 4:1–9; Matthew 22:1–14.

Lord God, shepherd of our souls,
   reviver of our spirits,
   guiding us in the right paths,

grant that we may fear no harm
   if we need to walk through a valley of deepest darkness,
for you will be with us
   and your goodness and love unfailing
      will follow us all the days of our lives.

You are truly a refuge to the needy in their distress,
   a shelter from the tempest and a shade from the heat.

For all nations you have prepared a banquet,
   a banquet of rich fare,
   a banquet of wines, well matured, strained clear,
   the feast for the wedding of your Son
      with the Church, the Bride of Christ.

Many have refused the invitation to come,
   and by your command we go out into the streets
      to invite everyone to the wedding.

Help us to be known to everyone
   for the consideration we give to others,
      even those serving other gods.

Hear our prayers and petitions,
   and our thanksgiving for your peace,
      which passes all understanding,
and let that peace
   guard our hearts and thoughts in Christ Jesus.

Proper 24

The Sunday between 16 and 22 October inclusive.

Continuous: Exodus 33:12–23; Psalm 99 (*or* Psalm 99:1–9) *or Related:*
Isaiah 45:1–7; Psalm 96:1–9, [10–13];
1 Thessalonians 1:1–10; Matthew 22:15–22.

Lord of the universe,
   maker of light and darkness,
author alike of well-being and woe in the order of creation,

King of Kings
   in your heavenly kingdom,
   attended by majesty and splendour,
   with might and beauty in your sanctuary.

We rejoice
   in the skies above,
     and the earth beneath,
   in the sound of the sea,
     and the creatures within it,
   in the fields
     with their crops,
   and in the trees of the forest,
     that shout for joy that the Lord is king.

We thank you for the fruits of the gospel,
   and pray that it may continue to spread,
     not by mere words,
     but in the strong conviction
       of the power of the Holy Spirit,
     taught in all sincerity as the way of life that you require.

Guide us to know where to draw the line
   between what belongs to human authority
     and what belongs to you,
and help us to pay our dues,
   as best we are able,
     to both divine and human authority.

Proper 25

The Sunday between 23 and 29 October inclusive.

Continuous: Deuteronomy 34:1–12; Psalm 90:1–6, 13–17 (*or* Psalm 90:1–6); *or Related:* Leviticus 19:1–2, 15–18; Psalm 1; 1 Thessalonians 2:1–8; Matthew 22:34–46.

Lord of us all,
  Lord of David,
    David's son,
God before creation and from age to age,
  daily mastering the millennia,
    like passing watches of the night,
and satisfying us at daybreak
  with love that makes us sing for joy,

You knew Moses face to face,
  filled him with the spirit of wisdom,
    and vouchsafed to him the Ten Commandments,
      which in essence were but two –
the first to love you with all our heart and soul and mind,
the second to love our neighbour as we love ourselves.

Yet we do not always like ourselves,
  even when we try to love our neighbour,
for we find ourselves seeking revenge,
  cherishing a grudge and nursing our disapprovals.

How far we are from total love for you,
  our God and Saviour.

In spite of assent in our minds,
  and inclination in our hearts,
    our worship so often lacks true soul.

Show us the whole land of our inheritance,
  the gospel of love and peace,
    and tempt us to possess it.

Bible Sunday

Nehemiah 8:1–4a, [5–6,] 8–12; Psalm 119:9–16; Colossians 3:12–17;
Matthew 24:30–35.

Lord of the thoughts of our minds,
   and of the inclinations of our hearts,
our teacher and tutor,
   testing us in our self-examination,
reveal to us the transcending truths
   of the scriptures,
      both old and new,

May today's expounders of your word
   read it with clarity,
   make plain its sense,
   and give instruction to those who can understand,
so that they may rejoice,
   as one rejoices over wealth of every kind,
      with feasting, and the sharing of feasting,
         because they have understood.

Throughout the ages of human awareness
   of divine activity in providential events,
we have recorded in scriptures
   beliefs as we knew them at those times.
You have, by continuing revelation,
   corrected our limited apprehension,
      until the fullest revelation was made
         in Jesus incarnate.

Teach us to teach one another
   with all the wisdom of your word,
      and with hymns and spiritual songs.

Teach us, also, through all the wisdom and beauty
   of the riches of poetry,
   of the uplifting images of art,
   and of the discoveries of science
      which resonate with your revelation.

Dedication Festival

The first Sunday in October or the last Sunday after Trinity.

1 Kings 8:22–30 (*or* Revelation 21:9–14); Psalm 122; Hebrews 12:18–24;
Matthew 21:12–16.

Lord in majesty,
  resplendent in mystery,
our imagination of your glory
  outstretches the capacity of our language.

Prophets and priests,
  and peoples of every kind,
have dedicated themselves to your service,
  and sought a sanctuary
    in which to sense your holiness.

The Temple in Jerusalem
  was a visible and tangible symbol,
    dedicated by the dedicated,
    securing the peace of the city
      in the promised Holy Land.

Bless the buildings in which we worship,
  make them known as houses of prayer,
    fountains of faith,
      and springs of the living water of hope.

Let the structures of stone and wood
  be signs of the new covenant mediated by Jesus,
  walls and pillars as spiritual support,
  windows to illuminate our minds,
  a font of cleansing and initiation,
  a lectern to make the Bible an open book,
  a pulpit for preaching and teaching,
  and an altar to focus your presence
    in tremendous and eternal mystery.

All Saints' Day

The Sunday between 30 October and 5 November inclusive or, if this is not kept as All Saints' Sunday, then 1 November itself.

Revelation 7:9–17; Psalm 34:1–10; 1 John 3:1–3; Matthew 5:1–12.

Lord of all the saints,
    on earth and in heaven,

With your angels encamped around the saints,
    a vast throng of all nations,
we worship you with thanksgiving,
    praising you for ever and ever
        for your glory and wisdom, honour, power and might.

You have called us your children and loved us as children.

What we shall be has not yet been disclosed,
    but we endeavour to make ourselves pure,
        grasping the hope
            that when Christ appears we shall be like him.

Give us grace to follow the eightfold way to divine happiness,
    knowing what it is
        to be poor in spirit,
        to mourn and be sorrowful,
        to be gentle and meek,
        to hunger and thirst to see right prevail,
        to show mercy,
        to be pure in heart,
        to be peacemakers,
        to be persecuted in the cause of right.

Bring us to taste and see that the Lord is good,
and set us free from all our fears,
    that we may be radiant with joy,
serving the Lamb upon the throne,
    Lamb become shepherd,
        guiding us to springs of the water of life.

The Fourth Sunday before Advent

*This is Proper 26 Alternative in RCL. The Sunday between 30
October and 5 November inclusive. For use if the feast of All Saints
was celebrated on 1 November and alternative propers are needed.*

Micah 3:5–12; Psalm 43 (*or* Psalm 107:1–8); 1 Thessalonians 2:9–13;
Matthew 24:1–14.

Lord our deliverer
  in times of misery and distress,
we praise you for your light and truth
  leading us to the altar
    of divine joy and awesome delight.

Guard us against false prophets,
  and those who entice us
    with the over-confidence
      of shallow understanding
        and expect to be rewarded.

Give us the patience
  to wait for your guidance
    in times of confusion,
and renew our trust in your power
  when the temples of our faith
    appear to be thrown down
      by those who mislead.

Speak to our needs
  through the loving care
    that others give us,
and restore our health of soul
  by the love we give to others
    in the strength and joy
      of your love for us.

The Third Sunday Before Advent

This is Proper 27 Alternative in RCL. The Sunday between 6 and 12 November inclusive.

Wisdom of Solomon 6:12–16; *Canticle*: Wisdom of Solomon 6:17–20 (*or* Amos 5:18–24; Psalm 70); 1 Thessalonians 4:13–18; Matthew 25:1–13.

Lord of all wisdom,
  the wisdom that shines brightly
    and never fades,

Rouse us in our search for wisdom
  from the sleep of ignorance,
    and lack of understanding,
      and let us not grow weary in our quest.

Develop our concern for learning
  into love of eternal wisdom,
    and determination to keep her laws,
and let the fear of the Lord
  that is the beginning of wisdom
    be replaced by the love of wisdom
      which leads us to love our Lord.

Let our vigilance in the cause of wisdom
  be the short and certain way
    to freedom from care
      by our trust in you.

Refresh our seeking
  with heavenly treasures found along the way,
    for which we rejoice and cry out
      'All glory to God!'

We know neither the day
  nor the hour of our death,
yet we can anticipate in our pilgrimage
  entry into the bedroom of the grave,
    in certain hope of being with Jesus.

The Second Sunday before Advent

This is Proper 28 Alternative in RCL. The Sunday between 13 and 19 November inclusive.

Zephaniah 1:7, 12–18; Psalm 90:1–8, [9–11,] 12 (*or* Psalm 90:1–8); 1 Thessalonians 5:1–11; Matthew 25:14–30.

Lord of the silence
  that makes the heart grow fonder,
    purifying our beliefs
      as we meditate on your presence,

Let us not be ruined by the complacency
  of excessive self-confidence,
    that prevents our growth towards maturity
      and frustrates the grace of the Spirit of Truth.

Make us know how few are our days,
  that our minds may learn wisdom
    and our hearts may be prepared for the day of the Lord.

In fighting for the right,
  keep us sober in our judgements,
    with faith and love our breastplate
      and the hope of salvation our helmet.

Help us to be trustworthy in small things,
  so that larger responsibilities may be placed upon us
    and bring us to our Master's joy.

Show the opportune occasions for us to encourage our neighbours,
  that we may build up one another
    and live in your company,
      and love one another as you love us.

By our freedom to repent
  you have destined us for the full attainment of salvation.

Help us to bring others to enjoy that same freedom
  and find their salvation,
    through our Lord Jesus Christ.

Christt the King

This is Proper 29 Alternative in RCL. The Sunday between 20 and 26 November inclusive.

Ezekiel 34:11−16, 20−24; Psalm 95:1−7a (*or* Psalm 95:1−7); Ephesians 1:15−23; Matthew 25:31−46.

Lord of Lords, and King of Kings,
　　royal shepherd to sheep of every nation,

You search for us when our days are dark,
　　and when clouds obscure our sight,
　　　　and you lead us to good pastures.

You bring us to health and strength,
　　so that we can relax and play together,
　　　　co-mingle and rest in safety.

Confer on us the spiritual gifts of wisdom and vision,
　　that lead to knowledge of you.

Let our inward eye be enlightened,
　　so that we may know the hope
　　　　to which we are called.

Reveal the vastness of the resources of your power
　　for those who have faith,
and bring us to recognize how supreme is your sovereignty,
　　commanding our allegiance,
　　　　and filling the whole universe.

Help us, your subjects, to be servants to one another
　　and to do for others what we would do for you,
and when at the last you separate sheep from goats,
　　and judge between
　　　　one sheep and another,
　　　　one goat and another,
grant, in your mercy, to remember
　　whatever good we have done for others,
　　　　which therefore we did for you,
　　　　　　however insignificant it may have seemed to be.

Harvest Thanksgiving

CLC p. 115. RCL: Thanksgiving Day. The fourth Thursday in November (USA) and the second Monday in October (Canada).

Deuteronomy 8:7–18 *or* 28:1–14; Psalm 65; 2 Corinthians 9:6–15; Luke 17:11–19.

Lord of the power to provide,
   with every need met to the full,
     and something to spare for every good cause,

Through our generosity will issue thanksgiving to God,
   and when those who receive join in prayer on our behalf,
     their hearts will go out to us
       because of the richness of the grace which you have given us.

You brought the Israelites to a good land,
   with streams and springs, and waters welling up in valley and hill.
A land with wheat and barley, vines, fig trees, olive oil and honey,
   rocks of iron ore, and hills for mining copper.

You warned them not to forget you
   by failing to keep your commandments.
And when they had plenty to eat, lived in fine houses,
   and had increasing herds, flocks, silver and gold,
     they were not to become proud and forgetful, nor say
'My own strength and energy have gained me this wealth.'

Grant that we may never forget that you love a cheerful giver,
   for he who sows sparingly reaps sparingly,
   and he who sows bountifully reaps bountifully.

How easy it is to receive from you,
   and be so pleased with the gift that we do not thank the giver.
Ten lepers were cleansed but only one turned back and gave thanks,
   and he was a Samaritan, to the Jews a foreigner.

We thank you for your care of the earth and for making it fruitful,
   for making open pastures lush, and hills wreathed in happiness,
     meadows clothed with sheep, and valleys decked with grain.
Everything breaks into song in praise of your bounty.

RCL: The Holy Name of Jesus

*Years A, B and C. CLC: The Naming and Circumcision of Jesus.
1 January.*

Numbers 6:22–27; Psalm 8; Galatians 4:4–7 (*or* Philippians 2:5–11 for
RCL); Luke 2:15–21.

Lord our sovereign,
  how majestic is your name throughout the world.

When we look at the moon and stars,
  what is a frail mortal that you should be mindful of him?
You have made him little less than God,
  master over all that you have made.

May the same mind be in us that was in Jesus,
  who was in the form of God,
    yet did not regard equality with God
      as something to be exploited.
He emptied himself, assuming the form of a slave,
  but God raised him to the heights,
    and bestowed on him the name above all names,
that at the name of Jesus every knee should bow,
  and every tongue acclaim,
    'Jesus Christ is Lord,'
      to the glory of God the Father.

Jesus was the name given by the angel before he was conceived,
    and sealed by circumcision
      eight days after his birth.

Mary treasured the message from the angels,
  announcing the birth of Messiah, the Lord,
    and pondered over its meaning.

Bless us, Lord, with the blessing for the Israelites:
  'May the Lord make his face shine upon us,
    and be gracious to us.
  May the Lord lift up his countenance upon us,
    and give us peace.'

RCL: New Year's Day

Years A, B and C. 1 January.

Ecclesiastes 3:1–13; Psalm 8; Revelation 21:1–6a; Matthew 25:31–46.

Lord of the ordering of our lives,
 everything has its season,
  and every activity under heaven has its time,
 a time to be born, and a time to die,
 a time to break down, and a time to build up,
 a time to weep, and a time to laugh,
 a time to mourn, and a time to dance,
 a time to seek, and a time to lose,
 a time to keep, and a time to throw away,
 a time for silence, and a time for speech,
 a time to love, and a time to hate,
 a time for war, and a time for peace.
You have made everything to suit its time.

We have been given a vision of a new heaven and a new earth,
 the Holy City, Jerusalem,
  made ready like a bride adorned for her husband.

The old order will have passed away,
 with its death, mourning, crying and pain,
  for all will be made new.

God will have his dwelling with mankind,
 and they shall be his people.

Grant that when the time comes to separate people, right and left,
 we may find ourselves on the right hand,
  destined for the kingdom, made ready since the world began.

Then we shall find that anything we did, for one of God's family,
 we did for God,
giving food and drink, taking strangers into our homes,
 providing clothes, helping the ill, and visiting those in prison.

Praise be to Alpha and Omega, our beginning and our end.

Lord For All Seasons

Year B

The First Sunday of Advent

Isaiah 64:1–9; Psalm 80:1–7, 17–19 (*or* Psalm 80:1–7); 1 Corinthians
1:3–9; Mark 13:24–37.

Lord of those who wait
    for the revelation of your power and glory,
        be it sooner or later,

No ear has heard,
    nor eye has seen,
        any other god who acts
            for those who wait for him.

You are our guardian and potter;
    we are like clay as your children,
        and all of us, in every way, are the work of your hand.

As shepherd of your flock,
    restore us to be in your image,
        making your face to shine upon us,
            that we may be saved.

We thank you, day by day,
    for your bountiful grace,
and for all of our enrichment in Christ,
    in speech and in knowledge
        of every kind.

What was testified to us about Christ
    has been amply confirmed
        in our experience
            of your faithfulness.

We await the day of final revelation,
    like the door-keeper of an empty house,
        awaiting his master's return.

Keep us awake and watching,
    and on our guard against intruders,
        for no one knows the day or hour
            of our Master's return.

The Second Sunday of Advent

Isaiah 40:1–11; Psalm 85:1–2, 8–13 (*or* Psalm 85:8–13); 2 Peter 3:8–15a;
Mark 1:1–8.

Lord of all time,
   its beginning and its end,

By days and years
   and thousands of years,
      you keep your promises.

Mortals flourish like the flowers of the field
   and by their nature fade and wither,
      but your word endures for ever.

Through the word of your prophets,
   a way was prepared,
   a highway across the desert,
      levelling the valleys and hills
         of stubborn self-seeking
            to reveal the glory of the Lord.

It is not your will that any should be lost,
   but that all should repent,
and be gathered into one flock,
   the lambs carried in your bosom,
      and the ewes led with gentleness.

We see deliverance near
   for those who worship you
      with steadfast love and faithfulness,
         embracing justice and peace.

John called us to repent
   and be baptized with water,
but you have brought us to the baptism with fire,
   by the Holy Spirit.

With eagerness we look forward
   to a new heaven and a new earth,
      in which righteousness is at home.

The Third Sunday of Advent

Isaiah 61:1–4, 8–11; Psalm 126 (*or Canticle*: Magnificat); 1 Thessalonians
5:16–24; John 1:6–8, 19–28.

Lord of all greatness,
   in whom our souls rejoice,

You fill the hungry with good things
   and have mercy on those that fear you.
You scatter the proud and all their scheming,
   and lift high the humble.

Your prophets were sent to announce good news,
   to bind up the broken-hearted,
   to proclaim liberty to captives,
   to comfort all who mourn,
   to give a garment of splendour
     for the spiritually depressed,
that they might all become
   like oaks of righteousness
     planted to display your glory.

Restore our fortunes, Lord,
   and renew our health,
fill our mouths with laughter
   and cause our tongues to sing with joy,
     for the riches of our harvest.

Grant that in continual prayer
   we may ever give thanks and praise,
     whatever our circumstances.

Lead us to discern,
   and never to stifle or neglect
     the inspiration and courage
       provided by the Spirit of Truth,

and help us to hold fast to what is good,
   and abstain from every form of evil,
     testifying to the true light
       of the gospel of peace.

The Fourth Sunday of Advent

2 Samuel 7:1–11, 16; *Canticle*: Magnificat (*or* Psalm 89:1–4, 19–26, *or* Psalm 89:1–8); Romans 16:25–27; Luke 1:26–38.

Lord of the divine mystery,
  kept in silence for long ages,
    but now disclosed and fulfilled,

Your command was made known to all nations,
  through prophetic writings,
    to bring them to faith and obedience.

For generation after generation,
  your ark of the covenant was housed in a tent,
    ready to journey with your people
      to their next dwelling-place.

And you were content,
  not desirous of a house of cedar
    or a temple of stone
until you could appoint a place for your people
  and plant the nation
    to be disturbed no more.

You fulfilled your covenant
  to establish their descendants for ever,
    and to hold their heads high,
      with yourself as the rock
        on which they find safety.

Then, at the appointed time,
  Mary, the most favoured one,
    was greeted by the archangel and told not to fear,
      for she would conceive and bear a son,
        Jesus, the Son of God.

May we become, like Mary, a living temple
  for the indwelling Saviour,
    Son of the Most High,
      who established for us
        the kingdom that has no end.

The First Sunday of Christmas

Isaiah 61:10 – 62:3; Psalm 148:1–14 (*or* Psalm 148:7–14); Galatians 4:4–7;
Luke 2:15–21.

Lord of our adoption
   as your children,
from a state of slavery to the whims of the world,
   we become heirs of the fortunes of your kingdom,
and receive the Spirit of your Son in our hearts.

You have clothed us in the robes of deliverance,
   and invested us with the regalia of victory,
like a garlanded bridegroom and a bride bedecked with jewels,
and we rejoice with all our hearts.

Praise and thanksgiving erupt in song,
   all creatures express their joy,
      birds of the air give melody,
      sea monsters share their rapture,
      wild animals and all cattle skip with pleasure,
      creeping creatures move with abandon,
      kings and commoners sing their chorus,
      young and old share their delight.

Such joy must have presaged events in Bethlehem.

Shepherds, in the fields, keeping watch,
   were terrified by an angel,
      announcing the birth of Messiah.

They hurried to find Mary and Joseph
   and the babe lying in the manger,
told of the message of the angel,
   astonishing all those who heard,
and returned to their flocks, glorifying and praising God.

But Mary treasured up all these things in her heart,
   and pondered over them.

May we too ponder the message of the angel,
   'A Saviour is born, who is the Messiah.'
      'Glory to God and peace on Earth.'

The Baptism of Christ

The First Sunday of Epiphany.

Genesis 1:1–5; Psalm 29; Acts 19:1–7; Mark 1:4–11.

Lord of the beginning of creation,
    and of its continuation throughout the ages
        until today,
           and tomorrow, if it be your will,

The sweep of the wind across the sea,
    and the glory of thunder,
        echo the power and majesty of your voice.

Your command, 'Let there be light'
    has still its primal power,
        dispelling the darkness that covers the depths
           of present-day despair.

In the baptism of John,
    a token of repentance for the forgiveness of sins,
that burden was removed
    and a commitment was made.

Crowds converged on John,
    inspired by the richness of his message,
undismayed by the poverty of his dress,
    a rough coat of camel's hair,
        and a leather belt about his waist,
nourished by the daily bread of his challenge,
    undeterred by his food of locusts and wild honey.

Grant that we may follow the example of humility set by Jesus
    who was himself baptized by John, doing God's will.

May the baptism into the name of the Lord Jesus
    open the way for greater gifts,
even as the laying on of hands
    by those possessing the Holy Spirit
        brought the Holy Spirit upon all believers.

The Second Sunday of Epiphany

1 Samuel 3:1–10, [11–20]; Psalm 139:1–6, 13–18 (*or* Psalm 139:1–10); Revelation 5:1–10; John 1:43–51.

Lord of our vocation,
   teach us how to listen to your call.

In these days, as in the days of Samuel,
   your word is rarely heard,
     and there is no outpouring of vision.

We need trustworthy prophets,
   with authority throughout our land,
     whose words will make tingle
       both of the ears of those who hear.

You are familiar with all the paths we take,
   you know us at rest and in action,
     and discern our thoughts from afar,
       and know all about the words we speak.

Wherever we go to flee from your presence, you are there,
   for darkness is not too dark for you,
     and night is as bright as day.

You fill us with awe, and we praise you,
   for we are fearfully and wonderfully made.

Your thoughts are full of mystery,
   and were we to try counting them,
     then to finish the count
       our years would need to equal yours.

In Jesus we find one who knows our thoughts,
   one who knew that in Nathanael
     there was no deceit, nothing false in him.
Jesus was the good thing that came,
   against all expectations, out of Nazareth.

May we persuade others, as Philip persuaded Nathanael,
   to come and see, and recognize
     the Son of God, King of Israel.

The Third Sunday of Epiphany

Genesis 14:17–20; Psalm 128; Revelation 19:6–10; John 2:1–11.

Lord of our obedience,
  when you make known your will,
    and we walk in your ways,

Abram followed your command,
  and you delivered his enemies into his power,
    so that he enjoyed the fruit of the labour of his hands.

Even in a vision your word can be made known,
    with the sound of a mighty throng,
    the roaring of a torrent,
    and the great peals of thunder,
calling us to rejoice and pay homage,
  for the wedding-day of the Lamb has come,
and happy are they who are invited
  to the wedding banquet, and to the worship of their God.

'Do whatsoever he tells you,'
  said Mary to the servants,
    and they obeyed.

'Fill jars with water,'
  said Jesus to the servants,
    and they did so, to the brim.

'Draw some off, and take it to the chief steward,'
  and they did so, and he was astonished and delighted,
    as he tasted what had been water.

And the bridegroom was congratulated
  for keeping the superior wine to the end
    when the inferior was the custom.

Teach us to know what to obey without question,
  what and how to question and consider,
    how to make up our minds,
      and how to be whole-hearted
        in obeying and refusing.

The Fourth Sunday of Epiphany

Deuteronomy 18:15–20; Psalm 111; Revelation 12:1–5a; Mark 1:21–28.

Lord in authority,
  making known your rules of action,
    precepts established to endure for ever,
  speaking through your prophets,
    and calling to account
      those who refuse to listen,

You have told us that heartfelt fear of the Lord,
  and respect for truth and justice,
    are the beginning of wisdom,
and those who live by these,
  and keep covenant with the Lord,
    grow in understanding.

Grant us a discerning awareness
  of the genuine among the false,
and instinctive recognition of the virtuous prophets
  among those that are deceived
    by their irreconcilable misunderstanding.

Lead us to delight in your words
  as we ponder over their meaning,
and make us patient and receptive
  when faced with the dramatic and mysterious
    in visions and dream-like imagination.

We too are amazed at your teaching,
  resonating to the note of authority
    that even the unclean evil spirit recognized
      as holy and full of healing power.

Guide us as we inwardly digest your message,
  and study, learn and respond to the gospel,
    so that we can transmit your truth
      by the power of the Spirit,
        to those who know you not.

Proper 1

The Sunday between 3 and 9 February inclusive (if earlier than the Second Sunday before Lent).

Isaiah 40:21–31; Psalm 147:1–11; 20c (*or* Psalm 147:1–11); 1 Corinthians 9:16–23; Mark 1:29–39.

Lord over the lords of the earth,
   from your throne above,
      the inhabitants of the world appear to be
         no more than grasshoppers.

You never weary, nor grow faint,
   your understanding is beyond us,
      in depths deeper than we can search.

Even the fittest of young men may stumble and fall,
but those who look to their Lord
   will win new strength,
   soar as on eagles' wings,
   run and not grow faint,
   march on and not grow weary,
      and will find pleasure
         in praising you for your steadfast love.

For Paul, it would have been agony
   if he had not preached the gospel,
      giving him well-earned satisfaction
         for simply discharging a trust.

Help us, like Paul, to become everyone's servant,
   and to be everything to everyone,
      to win over as many as possible.

We may not be able, like Jesus,
   to heal many and drive out demons,
yet we can follow his example,
   by rising in the morning when it is still very dark,
      and going to a remote spot to pray.

Proper 2

The Sunday between 10 and 16 February inclusive (if earlier than the Second Sunday before Lent).

2 Kings 5:1−14; Psalm 30; 1 Corinthians 9:24−27; Mark 1:40−45.

Lord our helper in times of trouble,
    turning mourning into dancing,
        stripping off sackcloth and clothing us with joy,

You cleansed the leper, Naaman,
    when he cooled his angry pride and learned humility from Elisha,
        by dipping himself seven times in Jordan.

It was a servant girl from Israel
    who gave word of Elisha to her mistress,
        witnessing to the power of his God;
it was a servant from Elisha who, by his message,
        unwittingly provoked the anger of Naaman;
it was the servants of Naaman who persuaded him
    to do the obvious thing, dissolving his arrogance.

We too know the power of your healing;
    when tears have lingered at nightfall
        rejoicing has come in the morning.

Jesus showed compassion to the trusting leper
    and immediately healed him with a touch,
        sternly warning him to tell no one but a priest;
yet he did, making public the whole story,
    so that the frustrated Jesus had to escape the crowds
        by hiding in the countryside.

Help us to strive, like athletes,
    who run against all the others in a race,
        in order to win a garland that perishes.
Let our real race be to bring our bodies under strict control,
    to win a garland that does not fade,
        lest after proclaiming to others
            we might find ourselves disqualified.

Proper 3

The Sunday between 17 and 23 February inclusive (if earlier than the Second Sunday before Lent).

Isaiah 43:18–25; Psalm 41; 2 Corinthians 1:18–22; Mark 2:1–12.

Lord of forgiveness and healing,
   wiping out our transgressions, remembering our sins no more.

We burdened you with our sins, and wearied you with our crimes,
but in your mercy you bid us
   to stop dwelling on past events, and brooding over days gone by.

You protect, and make happy,
   those who have concern for the poor and helpless,
and when those who visit them
   speak from hearts devoid of sincerity,
      and are keen to gather bad news,
         you uphold the sick because of their integrity.

All your promises were affirmed in Jesus,
   without mixture of 'Yes' and 'No'
      but with a resounding 'Yes',
         to which we say, 'Amen, in God we trust.'

The crowds that came to see Jesus in Capernaum found,
   like Mary and Joseph in Bethlehem,
      that there was no room in his house for them.
But the paralysed man, and his friends, were undeterred,
   broke through the roof, and lowered down the patient,
      showing their faith in Jesus.
'Your sins are forgiven,' said Jesus, with authority,
   offending the questioning scribes,
      and knowing at once what they were thinking,
         he added, 'Stand up, take your bed, and go home.'

Grant, Lord, that we may find forgiveness through our faith,
   be restored to health in our home on earth,
      and finally enter our home in heaven.

The Second Sunday before Lent

Proverbs 8:1, 22–31; Psalm 104:24–35; Colossians 1:15–20; John 1:1–14.

Lord of word and wisdom,
  voice of understanding,
    image of the invisible God,
      through whom all things came to be.

In the beginning, you already were,
  before the earth and the heavens,
  before the oceans, with the horizon like a girdle,
  before mountains settled in their place,
  before springs brimmed over with water,
    you were creating like a master-worker
      forever side by side with God.

You are the light of the world, for each and every season;
  your light can never be overcome by darkness
    and shines forever for all people.

They look to you in hope,
  to give them their food in due season,
and when you open your hand,
  they are filled with good things.

John testified to your light
  that everyone might believe,
and you became flesh,
  and made your home with us,
    but many did not recognize you.

Yet to those who put their trust in you
  comes the power and right
    to become children of God,
      and to see your glory,
        full of grace and truth.

Grant that we may recognize you
  as the origin and head of the Church,
    in whom the fullness of God chose to dwell,
    and through whom all was reconciled to God.

RCL: The Eighth Sunday after the Epiphany

The equivalent of the Second Sunday before Lent of CLC.

Hosea 2:14–20; Psalm 103:1–13, 22; 2 Corinthians 3:1–6; Mark 2:13–22.

Lord for all sinners,
   whom you call to be your disciples,
      with whom you dine regardless of the criticism of the scribes,

It is the sick that need a doctor, not the healthy;
   you did not come to call the virtuous but sinners.

You were like a bridegroom to your friends,
   and they provided a feast
      that you could not possibly refuse without causing offence,
even though disciples of John the Baptist were keeping a fast.
   The Pharisees likewise fasted, some of whom chose
      to make the occasion a cause for complaint.

How slow we are to bless you with all our being,
   and remember all your benefits.
You satisfy us with all good things in the prime of life,
   and our youth is renewed like an eagle's.

You have not treated us as our sins deserve,
   or repaid us according to our misdeeds.
As far as east is from west,
   so far from us you have put away our offences.

You wooed Israel when she was like a wanton wife,
   leading her into the wilderness
      to speak words of tender encouragement.
You restored her vineyards,
   turning the valley into a gate of hope,
      and sweeping weapons of war off the earth.

Grant that we need no letter of introduction to fellow believers,
   other than the letter you have given us to deliver,
      written not with ink but with your living Spirit,
         not on stone tablets but on the pages of the human heart.

The Sunday Next before Lent

2 Kings 2:1–12; Psalm 50:1–6; 2 Corinthians 4:3–6; Mark 9:2–9.

Lord of mysteries of sight and sound;
    Elijah's translation into heaven,
      and the transfiguration of Jesus, with a voice from a cloud,

Elisha, knowing that you were about to take Elijah away,
  pledged on his life that he would not leave him.
By invitation, and with boldness, Elisha made his wish,
  to inherit a double share of the spirit of Elijah,
and by his witness of the whirlwind,
    carrying up Elijah in chariots and horses of fire,
      his desire was fulfilled,
        and he assumed the cloak of Elijah.

On a high mountain, by themselves,
  Peter, James and John witnessed in terror
    the presence of Elijah and Moses,
      and the dazzling white clothes of Jesus,
      and knew not what to say.
But the voice in the cloud knew what to say:
  'This is my beloved Son, listen to him,'
    and suddenly only Jesus was with them.

Those that believed that Jesus was the light,
  shining out of the darkness of this world,
    gained knowledge of the glory of God in the face of Jesus,
    proclaiming Christ as Lord.

But those with unbelieving minds,
  being blinded by the god of this passing age,
    are on the way to self-destruction,
and the gospel of the glory of Christ,
  who is the image of God,
    cannot dawn on them and bring them light.

Grant, Lord, that we may share
  in the transfiguration of our souls,
    and in translation from the bonds of this world,
      by the grace of your Holy Spirit.

The First Sunday of Lent

Genesis 9:8–17; Psalm 25:1–10; 1 Peter 3:18–22; Mark 1:9–15.

Lord of the sacrament of baptism,
    symbolically received by Noah,
        according to tradition,
            when he was brought to safety
    through water and flood,

He divined significance in the rainbow,
    seen in rain and sun against a cloud,
        a covenant of promise
            never to flood the world again.

Baptism brings to us salvation
    through your suffering, once for all,
        and through your resurrection,
not as a washing of dirt from the body,
    but as an appeal to God for a good conscience.

After Jesus was baptized, the Spirit drove him
    into the wilderness
        to be tempted,
to ensure that he was well equipped
    to proclaim the good news
that the time had arrived,
    the kingdom of heaven had come near,
        it was time to repent
            and believe the gospel.

Lord, you lift our hearts and souls,
    and make your paths known to us.

All day long, we put our hope in you,
    for you guide the humble in right conduct,
        and bless us with your tender care
            and love unfailing.

The Second Sunday of Lent

Genesis 17:1–7, 15–16; Psalm 22:23–31; Romans 4:13–25; Mark 8:31–38.

Lord of the everlasting covenant
  made with Abram, the 'Exalted Ancestor',
    extending to a multitude of nations,
      renaming him Abraham, 'Ancestor of a Multitude',

His faith was tested by your promise of a son
  when he was nearly a hundred years old,
and his wife Sarai old enough to be a 'Mockery'.
  But blessed by a new name, Sarah, 'Princess',
    she was to become a mother of nations,
      from whom kings would spring.

Not through law was Abraham given the promise
  that he and his descendants
    would receive the world as their inheritance,
      but it was through righteousness that came through faith.

It was by faith, a matter of sheer grace,
  valid for all descendants,
    not only those who hold by the law,
so that our faith, like Abraham's,
  is to be counted to us as righteousness.

Jesus tried to teach his disciples
  that he must endure great suffering,
    be rejected and die, and rise again after three days.

Most did not understand,
  Peter took him aside and rebuked him,
    only to be in turn rebuked as devilish,
      thinking as men think and not as God thinks.

Grant that we may heed the words of Jesus,
  'Anyone who wants to follow me must renounce self,
    take up his cross and come with me,'
so that through our witness the coming generations
  shall be told, 'The Lord has acted.'

The Third Sunday of Lent

Exodus 20:1–17; Psalm 19:1–14 (*or* Psalm 19:7–14); 1 Corinthians 1:18–25; John 2:13–22.

Lord of the Ten Commandments,
   that give light to the eyes,
      revive the soul, and make the simple wise,

Grant us grace
   never to have another god before you,
   never to worship a graven image,
   never to misuse the name of God,
   never to break the holiness of the sabbath,
   never to dishonour father or mother,
   never to commit murder,
   never to commit adultery,
   never to steal,
   never to give false evidence against a neighbour,
   never to covet a neighbour's household.

Make us aware of our unwitting sins,
   cleanse us from secret faults,
      and let not wilful sins get the better of us.

The world failed to find you by wisdom alone,
   although the Greeks sought wisdom more than most,
    and were admired for their respect for things unseen,
      and for acknowledging 'the unknown God'.

The Jews asked for signs to believe in your promises,
   and even demanded one from Jesus
     to justify the cleansing of the Temple,

but no sign could persuade them
   except it be the resurrection of Jesus,
     Christ nailed to the cross,
      the power of God, and the wisdom of God,
sheer folly to those on the way to destruction,
   yet wiser than human wisdom,
     stronger than human strength,
      to those on the way to salvation.

The Fourth Sunday of Lent

Numbers 21:4–9; Psalm 107:1–3, 17–22 (*or* Psalm 107:1–9); Ephesians
2:1–10; John 3:14–21.

Lord of the gift of grace,
   whereby we are saved through faith,
      not by our own doing, not a reward for work done;
         for we have nothing to boast about.

For once we were spiritually dead,
   ruled by our carnal passions and physical desires,
      and did what instinct and evil imagination suggested,
         but you brought us to life with Christ.

For God so loved the world that he gave his only Son,
   that everyone who has faith in him
      may not perish but have eternal life.

It was not to condemn the world that God sent his Son,
   but so that through him the world might be saved,
      for the unbeliever is already condemned by his unbelief,
         preferring darkness to light, to hide his misdeeds.

We can understand the feelings of the Israelites
   as they journeyed to the promised land.
They grew impatient, bellyaching
   that they were heartily sick of the miserable food.
Bitten by snakes, smitten in their consciences for complaining,
      they cried to the Lord,
who ordered a graven image of a poisonous serpent
   to be made in bronze and erected as a standard
      so that those who looked at it recovered.

Some lost their way in the desert,
   some were fools who took to rebellious ways.
But when they cried to the Lord, the thirsty were satisfied,
   the hungry were filled with good things,
and they offered sacrifices of thanksgiving
   and told of his deeds with songs of joy.

May we, lost and foolish, be led safely home.

The Fifth Sunday of Lent

Passiontide begins.

Jeremiah 31:31–34; Psalm 51:1–12 (*or* Psalm 119:9–16); Hebrews 5:5–10;
John 12:20–33.

Lord of your humanity,
   Son of God in your divinity,
      you found your soul in torment
         when the hour had come for you to be glorified.

In human terms there was so much for you still to do,
   in divine terms there was but one thing to do,
      for this is what you came to do,
         to be lifted up from the earth,
            and draw everyone to yourself.

You were both victim, learning obedience through your sufferings,
and priest, designated by God a High Priest,
and source of eternal salvation for all who follow and obey you.

We know well our misdeeds,
   and our sins confront us all the time.
Be gracious to us in the abundance of your mercy,
   blot out our misdeeds, wash away all our iniquity,
   and cleanse us from our sin,
      that we may be whiter than snow.

Write your new covenant on our hearts,
   teach us wisdom in our secret hearts,
      and create pure hearts within us.

Grant that we may treasure your promise in our hearts,
   meditate on your precepts,
   keep your paths before our eyes,
   and not forget your word.

Restore to us the joy of your deliverance,
   and sustain in us lively and willing spirits.

Easter Day

Acts 10:34–43 (*or* Isaiah 25:6–9); Psalm 118:1–2, 14–24 (*or* Psalm 118:14–24); 1 Corinthians 15:1–11 (*or* Acts 10:34–43); John 20:1–18 (*or* Mark 16:1–8).

Lord of the resurrection,
  exchanging a tortured physical body
    for the transformed and spiritual body,
      still bearing the scars in hands, and feet, and side,

Like your disciples and the loyal women,
  we understand so little, and need to believe so much,
    and share with them the awe and wonder.

The two Marys and Salome ran away from the empty tomb,
  trembling with amazement,
    failing at first to obey the angel's command
      to tell Peter and the disciples,
        for they said nothing to anyone.

Peter and John, eventually told by Mary of Magdala, ran to the tomb,
  saw that it was empty, realised that Jesus must rise from the dead,
    and returned to their homes.

Last and, by his own admission, least,
  Paul saw Jesus on the road to Damascus,
    and in a vision like a precipitate birth he was born again.

He was what he was by God's grace,
  and laboured more than anyone to spread the gospel,
    first and foremost handing on the tradition
      that Christ died for our sins, was buried, and raised to life.

Grant that we may obey your command to testify to people,
  that everyone that believes in you
    receives forgiveness of sins
      through your name.

And let us sing aloud with thankful hearts,
  'This is the day that the Lord has made,
    let us rejoice and be glad in it.'

The Second Sunday of Easter

Acts 4:32–35; Psalm 133; 1 John 1:1 – 2:2; John 20:19–31. *(For those who require an Old Testament reading: Exodus 14:10–31; 15:20–21, to be read before the reading from Acts.)*

Lord of the evidence,
   of crucifixion, and of resurrection,

No longer can we find faith by seeing you here on earth,
   we cannot put our fingers into the place where the nails were,
     nor our hand into your side,
yet by your grace upon grace
   we believe and are happy.

You are the Word which gives life,
   present from the beginning,
     made visible on earth,
the God of light
   in whom is no darkness at all.

With great power, the apostles bore witness to the resurrection,
   and the whole company of believers
     was united in heart and soul,
       never a needy person among them.

How good and pleasant it is
   to live together as brothers in unity.
It is like fragrant oil poured on the head,
   and like dew falling on the mountains of Zion.

May we never claim to be sinless,
   for then the truth is not in us,
     and we deceive ourselves.
But rather let us confess our sins,
   for you may be trusted then to forgive us our sins,
     by your sacrifice for the sins of the whole world.

Breathe on us daily,
   that we may receive the Holy Spirit,
     and hear your greeting and your farewell,
       'Peace be with you.'

The Third Sunday of Easter

Acts 3:12–19; Psalm 4; 1 John 3:1–7; Luke 24:36b–48. *(For those who require an Old Testament reading: Zephaniah 3:14–20, to be read before the reading from Acts.)*

Lord of all peoples,
    how great is the love bestowed on us
        that we are called your children.

We grasp the hope that we shall be like Christ,
    doing what is right,
        making ourselves pure.

Peter was not surprised by the healing of a cripple,
    for he knew that the name of Jesus
        by awakening faith,
            gave strength to the man and healed him.

He told the crowd that by disowning Jesus before Pilate,
    when Pilate had decided to release him,
        and by reprieving a murderer,
            they had by their actions killed the Author of Life,
yet Peter told them he knew quite well that they acted in ignorance,
    as also did their rulers,
        and they needed only to repent of their sins
            and turn to God,
                that their sins might be wiped out.

Be gracious to us
    and hear our prayer,
let awe and wonder dispel our worries,
    and as we ponder in our beds
        help us to meditate in silence.

You have put into our hearts
    a greater happiness than others had,
        that trusted in grain and wine in plenty.

We can therefore lie down and sleep in peace,
    for it is you alone, Lord,
        who lets us live in safety.

The Fourth Sunday of Easter

Acts 4:5–12; Psalm 23; 1 John 3:16–24; John 10:11–18. (For those who require an Old Testament reading: Genesis 7:1–5, 11–18; 8:6–18; 9:8–13, to be read before the reading from Acts.)

Lord of love in action,
    love that is not a matter of theory or talk,
        but love that prepares us to give our lives for anyone in need,
even as Christ gave his life for us,
    that we might belong to the realm of truth,

Whenever our consciences condemn us, and we repent,
    then by God's grace we can reassure ourselves,
        for God is greater than our consciences
            and knows our wills and desires.

When our consciences do not condemn us,
    then we can approach God with confidence,
        making our requests known to him,
            certain that he dwells in us by his Spirit.

Both before a crowd, hungry to hear him,
    and before a disbelieving court of rulers,
        Peter gave a straight answer to the question
         'By what power, or by what name,
            have such men as you done this healing?'
Peter said, 'The answer is in the name of Jesus, whom you rejected,
    the name granted to people throughout the world
        by which mankind can be saved, and have life in all its fullness.'

You, Lord, are the good shepherd,
    laying down your life for the sheep,
not like a hired man who cares not for the sheep
    and who runs away when the wolf comes,
        so that the sheep are harried and scattered.

You know your sheep, and your own sheep know you.
Grant that other sheep, not belonging to your fold,
    will listen to your voice in our witness, and be led by you,
        so that there will then be one flock and one shepherd of us all.

The Fifth Sunday of Easter

Acts 8:26–40; Psalm 22:25–31; 1 John 4:7–21; John 15:1–8. *(For those who require an Old Testament reading: Baruch 3:9–15, 32 – 4:4 or Genesis 22:1–18, to be read before the reading from Acts.)*

Lord, the source of love,
  help us to love one another,
    and become children of God,
      and know God.

The truth of the matter is that you first loved us
  so that we might have life through you.

In love there is no room for fear –
  indeed, perfect love banishes fear,
    for fear has to do with punishment,
      and the forgiven are not punished.

If we do not love fellow Christians whom we have seen,
  we are surely incapable of loving God, whom we have not seen.

A vine-grower who loves his vine
  cuts away the barren branches,
    and prunes clean the fruiting branch
      to make it more fruitful still.

You are the vine and we are the branches,
  and we can bear fruit only if we remain united with the vine.

If we dwell in you, and your words dwell in us,
  then whatever we ask will be so acceptable to you,
    that you will grant our request.

How can we understand what we read
  in the prophets and the rest of holy Scripture
    without someone to guide us?

Send us a Philip of our time
  to tell us more of the good news of the gospel,
    and send us on our way rejoicing,
      praising you for our deliverance.

The Sixth Sunday of Easter

Acts 10:44–48; Psalm 98; 1 John 5:1–6; John 15:9–17. *(For those who require an Old Testament reading: Isaiah 55:1–11, to be read before the reading from Acts.)*

Lord of true friendship,
   for those who obey your commands,
      commands that are not burdensome,

To the disciples, your friends, you disclosed
   everything made known by God.

Your love makes our joy complete,
   for there is no greater love than yours,
      love that led you to lay down your life for your friends.

We did not choose you:
   you chose us,
      and appointed us to bear fruit by witnessing,
         fruit that will last.

Those who listened to the message of Peter
   received the gift of the Holy Spirit,
      and spoke with tongues of ecstasy,
and circumcized believers, men of Jewish birth,
   were amazed that the gift of the Holy Spirit
      was poured out on Gentiles.

Grant that we may never be so prejudiced
   that we are surprised
      by the working of your Holy Spirit.

Your victory over sin
   is made known to every nation,
      and throughout the earth
         new songs are sung to the Lord,
psalms are sung to your honour,
   with lyre and trumpet, and echoing horn,

and our thanksgiving is heard in the sounds of lapping waters
   as the rivers clap their hands.

The Seventh Sunday of Easter

The Sunday after Ascension Day.

Acts 1:15–17, 21–26; Psalm 1; 1 John 5:9–13; John 17:6–19. *(For those who require an Old Testament reading: Ezekiel 36:24–28, to be read before the reading from Acts.)*

Lord of the unity of Father and Son,
   protect us by the power of your name,
      that we may be one, as you are one.

Let us take note of your words
   so that your joy may be within us in full measure,
   and we may know with certainty
      that you were sent to teach us
         all that you received from the Father.

Make us strangers to the evil of this world,
   even as you were in your life on earth,
      and consecrate us by the truth of your word.

Human testimony is all around us,
   but believing in you as Son of God
      brings testimony into our own hearts.

May we never take the counsel of the wicked for a guide,
   or join in the company of scoffers,
but let us delight in the law of the Lord
   and make it our meditation day and night,
that we might be like trees near streams of water
   whose foliage never fades, whose fruit is abundant in due season.

You know the hearts of everyone, Lord,
   and choose those to receive the office of ministry,
even as you chose Matthias to be an apostle
   to join the eleven when Judas forfeited his place.

Give us grace sufficient to the day
   that we may join with your ministers
      in witnessing to the power and glory of your resurrection.

The Day of Pentecost

Whit Sunday.

Acts 2:1–21 (*or* Ezekiel 37:1–14); Psalm 104:24–34, 35b (*or* Psalm 104:24–35); Romans 8:22–27 (*or* Acts 2:1–21); John 15:26–27; 16:4b–15. *The reading from Acts must be used as either the first or second reading.*

Lord of Pentecost,
    the day when we celebrate the first fruits of harvest,
        fifty days since the rising to life of the buried seed,

You did not leave us helpless,
    but sent an advocate, the Spirit of Truth,
        so that we might testify on your behalf.

There was so much more to be told by you,
    but the burden would have been too great for the disciples,
        until the Spirit of Truth arrived
            to guide them, and us, into all truth, throughout the ages.

Ezekiel, carried away by the Spirit,
    saw Israel as a pile of dry bones,
        countless in number, lying in a valley.
To the question 'Can these bones live?' he replied,
    'Only you, Lord, know that,'
and he heard in his imagination
    the rattling together of the bones,
        fitting themselves together, bone to its bone,
and he saw, in his mind's eye, their complete enfleshment
    and their endowment with life,
        as a promise of the restoration of Israel.

Grant that we too may be restored by an outpouring of the Spirit,
and let the inarticulate groans of our attempts to pray,
    and the efforts of our meditations,
        be interpreted by the Spirit
            as you search out our inmost being.

Trinity Sunday

Isaiah 6:1−8; Psalm 29; Romans 8:12−17; John 3:1−17.

Lord of threefold glory,
   holy, holy, holy,
     the whole earth is full of your glory.

The voice of the Lord echoes over the waters,
   the voice of power, and full of majesty,
     giving strength to your people
       and blessing them with peace.

We live among people who have unclean lips,
   insensitive to lies and deceit,
     unaware of their profanities,
and we know that we too are not blameless in our speech.

Let an angel's painful touch
   of a glowing coal on our unguarded lips
     wipe out our sin and win for us new strength,
that when you, Lord, seek for someone to witness for you
   we may reply, 'Here I am, send me.'

Our witness is that God so loved the world
   that he gave his only Son,
     that everyone who has faith in him
       may not perish but have eternal life.

Nicodemus respected Jesus as a teacher,
   and by many signs knew that he was sent by God,
     yet he did not understand the need to be born again,
       from water and Spirit.

The Spirit gives birth to spirit,
   and we do not know where it has come from,
     nor where it is going,
       but everyone who has faith has eternal life.

May we by the Spirit of God, as sons of God, cry 'Abba, Father,'
   and as his children become joint heirs with Christ.

Proper 4

The Sunday between 29 May and 4 June inclusive (if after Trinity Sunday).

Continuous: 1 Samuel 3:1–10, [11–20]; Psalm 139:1–6, 13–18; *or Related:* Deuteronomy 5:12–15; Psalm 81:1–10; 2 Corinthians 4:5–12; Mark 2:23 – 3:6.

Lord of the sabbath,
   the day made for our rest,
      free us from over-confidence
         in distinguishing right from wrong,
            in matters of tradition,

Heal the withered arm of our imagination,
   whatever the day of the week,
      and look not with anger and sorrow
         when silence betrays our obstinate stupidity.

When you speak to us may you find us not merely hearing,
   as Samuel did, the first three times,
      but listening, with expectation,
         ready to respond to your call.

You know us so well, at rest and in action,
and guard us behind and before, steadying us with your arm.

We praise you for your wonderful works,
   and raise a melody with tuneful lyre and harp,
      beating the tambourine and blowing the trumpet.

You have caused light to shine in our hearts,
   the knowledge of the glory of God,
yet we are but earthenware pots
   holding this treasure of transcendent power.

Grant that when we are afflicted, perplexed and hunted,
   we will never feel cornered, driven to despair, or forsaken,
      for you are our shield and defender.

Proper 5

The Sunday between 5 and 11 June inclusive (if after Trinity Sunday).

Continuous: 1 Samuel 8:4–11, [12–15,] 16–20; [11:14–15]; Psalm 138; *or*
Related: Genesis 3:8–15; Psalm 130;
2 Corinthians 4:13 – 5:1; Mark 3:20–35.

Lord of abounding grace,
   shared more and more when we believe and witness,
so that a greater chorus of thanksgiving
   rises to the glory of God,

Eternal glory far outweighs present troubles,
   provided we fix our eyes on things unseen,
     for things seen are transient,
       things unseen are eternal.

Our souls wait for you, Lord,
   more eagerly than watchmen waiting for the morning,
     for your love and forgiveness are unfailing,
       making the lowly bold and strong in soul.

May your kingdom never be divided,
   lest it fail to withstand the evil around and within us.

When we feel like the elders of Israel,
   determined to have a king,
     unaware of the dangers of corruption
       in the unbridled use of power,
turn us to Jesus as our king,
   and guard us against the confusion
     between divine and devilish power,
       lest we blaspheme against your Holy Spirit.

Assist us in our relationships with friends and family,
   discerning the wisdom of the saying of Jesus,
     'Whoever does the will of God
       is my brother and sister and mother.'

Proper 6

The Sunday between 12 and 18 June inclusive (if after Trinity Sunday).

Continuous: 1 Samuel 15:34 – 16:13; Psalm 20; *or Related:* Ezekiel 17:22–
24; Psalm 92:1–4, 12–15 (*or* Psalm 92:1–8);
2 Corinthians 5:6–10, [11–13,] 14–17; Mark 4:26–34.

Lord, you do not see as mortals see,
  observing only the apppearances, for you see into the heart.

Whether it be selecting a king, or a prophet,
  or a disciple to proclaim the gospel, your criteria stand the test.

Samuel, grieving still at the disappointing reign of King Saul,
  feared for his life when God sent him to Jerusalem
    to anoint a new king from among the sons of Jesse.
The elders trembled at his approach, asking,
  'Do you come peaceably?' and heard, 'All is well.'

Seven sons were rejected and the youngest was chosen,
  David, pure in heart, and handsome.

With faith as our guide, unceasingly confident,
  we know that our lives must be laid open
    before the tribunal of Christ.

May we, in our heart of hearts, be open to God,
  and also be aware of our true selves.
For worldly standards should have ceased to count
  in our estimate of anyone,
    since anyone united to Christ is a new creation.

The kingdom of God is like seed that produces a good harvest.
Again, from the smallest of seeds, mustard grows to the tallest plant,
  and birds roost in the shade of its branches.
With such parables you taught the people,
  explaining everything privately to your disciples.

It is good to give thanks to you,
  for great are your deeds
    and your thoughts are very deep.

Proper 7

The Sunday between 19 and 25 June inclusive (if after Trinity Sunday).

Continuous: 1 Samuel 17:[1a, 4–11, 19–23] 32–49; Psalm 9:9–20; (*or*
1 Samuel 17:57 – 18:5, 10–16; Psalm 133); *or Related:* Job 38:1–11; Psalm
107:1–3, 23–32 (*or* Psalm 107:23–32);
2 Corinthians 6:1–13; Mark 4:35–41.

Lord of enduring love,
  caring for those in trouble or distress,

That was not remembered by your disciples on the lake,
  who woke you and complained,
    'Teacher, do you not care that we are sinking?'
You rebuked the wind and waves, 'Peace, be still,'
  and rebuked the disciples, 'Why such cowards? Have you no faith?'
  And all they could say was, 'Who can this be?'

Did the Philistines ask that same question concerning David
  when he cut off Goliath's head?
    Or did they come to acknowledge
      the might of the God of Israel?

Nations have plunged into a pit of their own making,
  and have entangled their feet in nets they have hidden,
    peoples have been trapped in their own devices.
Lord, let the nations know that they are but human beings,
  and Lord, as our tower of strength, restrain the power of mortals.

Job was challenged to brace himself, and stand up like a man.
  Where was he when you laid the earth's foundation,
    and who fixed its dimensions and set its corner-stone in place
      while the morning stars sang in chorus,
        and all the sons of God shouted for joy?

Grant that in our sorrows we always have cause for joy,
  liberated from the tensions of guilt,
    and uplifted by whole-hearted thankfulness.

Proper 8

The Sunday between 26 June and 2 July inclusive.

Continuous: 2 Samuel 1:1, 17–27; Psalm 130; *or Related:* Wisdom of Solomon 1:13–15; 2:23–24; Canticle: Lamentations 3:23–33 (*or* Psalm 30); (*Lamentations 3:23–33 may be read as the first reading in place of Wisdom 1:13–15; 2:23–24*).

2 Corinthians 8:7–15; Mark 5:21–43.

Lord of all that we have,
  we wait for you patiently.

When the yoke that we bear in our youth is too heavy,
  it is good for us to sit in silence,
    for you do not willingly grieve any mortal.
Your love and compassion are new every morning,
  so great is your constancy, and your power to deliver.

David's loving lament for Saul and Jonathan
  stirs the hearts of every generation:

'Beloved and lovely were Saul and Jonathan,
  neither in life nor in death were they parted,
    swifter than eagles, stronger than lions.
Jonathan, your love for me was wonderful,
  surpassing the love of women.'

Paul appealed to the love of the Corinthians,
  who were so rich in everything,
    in faith, speech, knowledge and diligence.
If we help others one day, then one day they will help us;
  'Those who gathered more, did not have too much,
  and those who gathered less, did not have too little.'

It was faith that healed the woman with a haemorrhage
  when she touched the clothes of Jesus.
Jesus sensed the flow of power and sought the cause,
  and she fell at his feet and told the whole truth.

May we ever tell the whole truth, and be healed,
  and be told, 'Go in peace.'

Proper 9

The Sunday between 3 and 9 July inclusive.

Continuous: 2 Samuel 5:1−5, 9−10; Psalm 48; *or Related:* Ezekiel 2:1−5;
Psalm 123;
2 Corinthians 12:2−10; Mark 6:1−13.

Lord of the answers
    to so many of our questions, yet there are so many questions
    to which we have no answers,

Paul knew a Christian, perhaps it was himself,
    caught up as far as the third heaven, and paradise,
        whether in the body or out of the body he did not know.
He heard secret words, unrepeatable on human lips,
    but did not boast, though it would be speaking the truth,
        not wanting anyone to form an estimate of him
            going beyond the evidence of their own eyes and ears.

It was in weakness that he was strong, for you, Lord, had told him,
    'My grace is all you need, power is most fully seen in weakness.'

The crowd in the Nazareth synagogue heard Jesus in amazement, asking,
    'Where does he get it from?'
    'What is this wisdom he has been given?'
    'How does he perform such miracles?'
        knowing him only as the carpenter's son
            with four brothers, and also sisters.
So they took offence at him;
    'A prophet never lacks honour except in his home town,
        and among his relations and in his home.'

And with that as a warning, he sent out the Twelve, two by two,
    taking nothing but a stick, sandals, one coat,
        no bread, no pack, no money,
proclaiming the need for repentance,
    anointing many sick people, and curing them.

Our eyes turn to you, Lord; be our guide for evermore,
    and help us to ponder on your steadfast love.

Proper 10

The Sunday between 10 and 16 July inclusive.

Continuous: 2 Samuel 6:1–5, 12b–19; Psalm 24; *or Related:* Amos 7:7–15;
Psalm 85:8–13;
Ephesians 1:3–14; Mark 6:14– 29.

Lord, you were seen by Amos
   with your plumb-line in your hand,
      showing how far from upright were your people,
         and warning of the fall of Israel.

You chose your people Israel, and now you have chosen us,
   that we may be without blemish
      and full of your gracious gift of love.

John the Baptist, good and holy, impressed Herod,
   but he was greatly disturbed
      when John told him he had no right
         to marry his brother's wife.

And the wiliness of the women,
   and the weakness of the man for woman,
      contrived to lead to the death of John,
         forerunner of your message of salvation and grace.

In the richness of your grace,
   you have lavished on us wisdom and insight,
      making known the mystery of your will,
         your secret purpose for the universe
            to be brought into unity in Christ.

Now we have believed the message of truth,
   stamp us with the seal of the Holy Spirit,
      a pledge of our inheritance
         when God liberates his own, to his glory and praise.

May your plumb-line ever find us
   upright in heart.

Proper 11

The Sunday between 17 and 23 July inclusive.

Continuous: 2 Samuel 7:1–14a; Psalm 89:20–37; *or Related:* Jeremiah 23:1–6;
Psalm 23;
Ephesians 2:11–22; Mark 6:30–34, 53–56.

Lord of Jew and Gentile,
  made one in union with Christ Jesus, a single new humanity,
    created by the annulment of the law,
      with its rules and regulations,

Gentiles are no longer aliens in a foreign land,
  but fellow-citizens with the saints,
    members of God's household,
      being built with all the others
        into a spiritual dwelling for God.

You promised David that your arm would give him strength,
  and that no enemy would outwit him,
    so that through your name he would hold his head high.
If his children forsook your law, you would punish them,
  but you would not violate your covenant,
    nor alter what you had promised.

As a shepherd you lead us to waters where we may rest,
  even as Jesus did with his disciples,
    taking them to a remote place to rest awhile,
      and to revive their souls.

Goodness and mercy followed you, everywhere and always,
  crowds gathered to hear you and to touch you,
    and you had compassion on them,
      for they were like sheep without a shepherd,
        and you taught them, and healed them.

Grant that we too may be as shepherds,
  not letting your sheep scatter by not watching over them,
    for we know that you are watching over us.

Proper 12

The Sunday between 24 and 30 July inclusive.

Continuous: 2 Samuel 11:1–15; Psalm 14; *or Related:* 2 Kings 4:42–44; Psalm 145:10–18;
Ephesians 3:14–21; John 6:1–21.

Lord, you support all who stumble,
    responding to all who raise their eyes to you in hope,
        giving them their needs in due season,
for you are close to all who call on you with sincerity.

Impious fools say in their hearts, 'There is no God.'
    Have they no understanding when no one does good,
        when unfaithfulness and corruption,
            depravity and wicked deeds, abound unchecked?

Kneeling in prayer, we ask you to grant
    inward strength and power through the Spirit,
        out of the store of treasures and glorious splendour
            of your everlasting kingdom.

Enable us to have deep roots and firm foundations
    so that we may be strong to grasp
        the breadth and length, height and depth of Christ's love,
            and to know it, though it is beyond knowledge.

May we be filled with all the fullness of God,
    and give glory to him who is able through his power
        to do immeasurably more than all we can ask or imagine.

Lord, let us never underestimate what you can do.
Let us rather seek the significance of what was believed
    by the observers and the recorders of miracles.

Above all you showed your care for the needy,
    you accepted what there was available,
        and made the most of it, giving thanks to the Father,
not forgetting to gather up the remnants
    so that nothing was wasted, no lazy litter left around.

Proper 13

The Sunday between 31 July and 6 August inclusive.

Continuous: 2 Samuel 11:26 – 12:13a; Psalm 51:1–12; *or Related:* Exodus 16:2–4, 9–15; Psalm 78:23–29;
Ephesians 4:1–16; John 6:24–35.

Lord of our hunger and thirst,
  you are the true bread of life;
    whoever believes in you will never be hungry or thirsty.

Moses and Aaron mediated the manna in the wilderness,
  with flesh to eat between dark and dusk.
Mortals ate of the bread of angels, grain from heaven,
  meat rained down like dust-storms of flying birds,
    and the people were well filled – just what they wanted.

David killed Uriah by the Ammonites' swords, and stole his wife.
  The prophet Nathan told a story of a rich man with many sheep
    who served up a poor man's only lamb for a traveller,
      evoking the angry condemnation of David,
        and Nathan's unavoidable accusation, 'You are the man,'
with David's subsequent confession, 'I have sinned against the Lord.'

Lord, be gracious to us, for our sins confront us all the time.
  Create in us clean hearts, and give us a new and steadfast spirit.
You desire faithfulness and truth in our inmost being,
  so teach us wisdom in our secret hearts.

Help us to live up to our calling, to be humble, gentle and patient,
  putting up with one another's failings in the Spirit of love,
    sparing no effort to make fast with bonds of peace
      the unity which the Spirit gives,
one in body, Spirit and hope, one faith, one baptism,
  one God and Father of us all, over all, through all and in all.

Grant that each person's special gifts may build up the Body of Christ,
  until we attain maturity, nothing less than the full stature of Christ,
    no longer children whirled around by gusts of new doctrines.

Proper 14

The Sunday between 7 and 13 August inclusive.

Continuous: 2 Samuel 18:5–9, 15, 31–33; Psalm 130; *or Related:* 1 Kings 19:4–8; Psalm 34:1–8;
Ephesians 4:25 – 5:2; John 6:35, 41–51.

Lord of the mysteries of bread from heaven,
   for you are that bread,
     sent from the Father,
       who draws us to believe in you,

The bread which you give is your own flesh,
   given for the life of the world,
that we might taste and see that the Lord is good,
   setting us free from all our fears, providing a refuge and hope.

Grant that we may never grieve you,
   nor offend against the Holy Spirit.

Help us to guard our lips against falsehood,
   and speak only that which is good and helpful to the occasion.

If we are angry, let it not lead us into sin,
   nor let sunset find us still nursing our anger.
Banish all spite, bad temper and malice of any kind,
   and guard us against rage, insults and slander.

Make us kind to one another, tender-hearted,
   forgiving one another as you forgive us,
     in a phrase – make us imitators of God.

Look with compassion on those who mourn,
   as did David for Absalom:
'O my son, Absalom my son, my son Absalom,
   Would that I had died instead of you,
     O Absalom, my son, my son.'

Lord, out of the depths we call upon you,
   let your ears be attentive to our supplication.

Proper 15

The Sunday between 14 and 20 August inclusive.

Continuous: 1 Kings 2:10–12; 3:3–14; Psalm 111; *or Related:* Proverbs 9:1–6; Psalm 34:9–14;
Ephesians 5:15–20; John 6:51–58.

Lord of our hearts and minds,
   fulfil in us the dream of Solomon.
Grant us thankful hearts with skill to listen,
   and understanding minds,
      with ability to distinguish good from evil.

Invite us to the feast of wisdom, with those that are simple,
   that eating the bread prepared,
      and the wine that is blended and spiced,
we may learn that the fear of the Lord is the beginning of wisdom,
   so that we advance in understanding
      and live and walk in the way of insight.

As children we listen to you teaching the fear of the Lord;
   keep our tongues from evil and our lips from telling lies,
      help us to shun evil and do good, seek peace and pursue it.

Grant us to understand what the will of the Lord is,
   taking care to behave sensibly,
      and to use present opportunities to the full.

Enrich our imagination concerning your flesh and blood,
   knowing that you did indeed sacrifice yourself,
      and sanctified the symbols of bread and wine.

When we eat and drink in remembrance of you
   we know that we dwell in you and you dwell in us,
and in very truth these are signs and symptoms
   that we have partaken of yourself
      in the similitude of bread and wine.
And we sing and make music in our hearts,
   giving thanks every day for everything
      in the name of our Lord Jesus Christ.

Proper 16

The Sunday between 21 and 27 August inclusive.

Continuous: 1 Kings 8:[1, 6, 10–11,] 22–30, 41–43; Psalm 84; *or Related:*
Joshua 24:1–2a, 14–18; Psalm 34:15–22;
Ephesians 6:10–20; John 6:56–69.

Lord of our battle against evil,
   source of all our strength, provider of our armour and defence,

Fasten on us the belt of truth,
   make integrity our breastplate,
    and let our shoes be the gospel of peace.
Provide the great shield of faith,
   and the helmet of salvation,
     with the word of God as the sword of the Spirit.

Our struggle is not against human foes
   but against the evil all around us,
     calling for constancy in prayer, keeping watch, and perseverance.

Your eyes, Lord, are on the righteous,
   and your ears are open to their cry.
You are close to those whose courage is broken,
   and you save those whose spirit is crushed.

How dearly loved was the Temple of your dwelling,
   the whole being of the Psalmist cried out with joy.
It was better for him to spend one day in your courts
   than a thousand days elsewhere.

It is the Spirit that gives life – the flesh can achieve so little,
   and whoever eats the bread of life will live for ever.
This difficult teaching was more than the disciples could stand,
   and an invitation to consider the ascension of the Son of Man
    led many to draw back.
When asked, 'Do you also want to leave?' Peter answered,
   for the twelve and for us, 'Lord, to whom shall we go?
    We believe and know that you are God's Holy One.'

Proper 17

The Sunday between 28 August and 3 September inclusive.

Continuous: Song of Solomon 2:8–13; Psalm 45:1–2, 6–9 (*or* Psalm 45:1–7); *or Related:* Deuteronomy 4:1–2, 6–9; Psalm 15;
James 1:17–27; Mark 7:1–8, 14–15, 21–23.

Lord of the beloved
   bounding over the mountains to his darling,
   leaping like a gazelle or a young stag,
      for winter is past and the rains are over,
      the season of flowers and bird-song is come,
      the turtle-dove's wooing is heard in the land,
      figs ripen and vine blossoms give forth their fragrance,
Rise up, my darling, my fair one, come away.

The Psalmist was astir with a noble theme, in honour of the king,
   his tongue ran swiftly like the pen of an inspired scribe.
'You surpass all others, gracious words flow from your lips,
   you advance in pomp and splendour, for truth and justice,
   enthroned by God with the royal sceptre of equity,
   anointed with fragrant oil as a token of joy,
   resonating with gladness to the music of strings.'

Joshua charged the people to observe carefully the commandments,
   so that they would display wisdom and discernment.
They were not to forget things seen with their own eyes,
   and were to teach them to children and to children's children.

One who leads a blameless life speaks the truth from his heart,
   has no malice, tells no tales against his neighbour,
   honours those who fear the Lord, never accepts a bribe,
   and holds to his oath even to his own hurt.

With you, Lord, there is no variation, no play of passing shadows.
   We must be quick to listen, slow to speak and slow to be angry.

Give us wisdom to review the ancient traditions of men,
   such as those concerning what and how we eat.

May we listen to the continuing revelation of the Spirit of Truth.

Proper 18

The Sunday between 4 and 10 September inclusive.

Continuous: Proverbs 22:1–2, 8–9, 22–23; Psalm 125; *or Related:* Isaiah
35:4–7a; Psalm 146;
James 2:1–10, [11–13,] 14–17; Mark 7:24–37.

Lord of both rich and poor,
    you judge esteem to be better than silver and gold,
        and a good name to be more desired than great riches.

Those who trust in you cannot be shaken,
    for you do good, Lord, to the good,
        and bless those who are generous and kindly.

To the anxious you say, 'Be strong, fear not,
    your God comes to rescue you,'
the blind see, deaf hear, lame leap like deer, the dumb sing for joy,
    water springs up in the wilderness,
        the mirage in the desert becomes a pool.

Grant that we may ever be impartial,
    and that we may never discriminate unfairly,
        and never judge by the uncertain standards of poverty and riches,
            by favouring a person with gold rings and fine clothes,
                and despising a poor person in dirty clothes.

You have chosen to make rich in faith
    those who are poor in the eyes of the world,
and you commend as excellent those who really fulfil the royal law,
    'Love your neighbour as yourself.'

Yet what good is it for us to say we have faith
    if our actions do nothing to show it? –
        for faith without works is dead.

You could not resist the Gentile woman with a sick daughter,
    who pleaded for the scraps left under the table
        by the children of Israel.
No wonder your fame spread, for all that you did, you did well.

Proper 19

The Sunday between 11 and 17 September inclusive.

Continuous: Proverbs 1:20–33; Psalm 19:1–14 (*or* Psalm 19:1–6; *or Canticle*: Wisdom of Solomon 7:26 – 8:1); *or Related:* Isaiah 50:4–9a; Psalm 116:1–9;
James 3:1–12; Mark 8:27–38.

Lord, by the word of your wisdom
   may we respond to your reproof,
      be filled with your Spirit, and share your thoughts,
lest we suffer terror like a hurricane,
   calamity like a whirlwind,
      and anguish and distress,
like those who sought you eagerly but failed to find you
   because they would not accept what they knew to be true,
      being solely concerned with their own conceits.

The stars tell out your glory, days and nights commune in silence,
   governed by the laws of your universe.

Your commandments give light to the eyes and revive the soul,
   yet we ignore our unwitting sins,
      and need to be cleansed of our secret faults,
         and granted a new taste of wisdom.

Wisdom is the radiance that streams from everlasting light,
   the flawless mirror of the active power of God,
      and the image of his goodness.

All of us go wrong, again and again,
   and need wisdom to make all things new.
Give us grace to tame our tongues,
   lest we praise you with one breath
      and curse fellow humans with the next,
or parallel Peter, who first confessed you as Messiah
   and then rebuked you for the plain speaking that predicted
      your suffering, your death and your rising again.

May the words of our mouths and the meditations of our hearts
   be acceptable to you, Lord, our rock and deliverer.

Proper 20

The Sunday between 18 and 24 September inclusive.

Continuous: Proverbs 31:10–31; Psalm 1; *or Related:* Wisdom of Solomon
1:16 – 2:1, 12–22 (*or* Jeremiah 11:18–20); Psalm 54;
James 3:13 – 4:3, 7–8a; Mark 9:30–37.

Lord, who can find a good wife?
  Her husband's whole trust is in her, and she sets about her work
    to bring him good all the days of her life.
  She is open-handed to the poor,
    and reaches out her hands to the needy.
  She is clothed in strength and dignity,
    and can afford to laugh at tomorrow.
  Charm is deceptive and beauty fleeting,
    but the woman who fears the Lord is honoured.

Wisdom from above is pure and peace-loving,
  considerate, open-minded, straightforward and sincere,
  rich in compassion and deeds of kindness.

Grant that the wise and learned prove themselves in practice
  by right conduct, with the modesty that comes of wisdom.

Peace is the seed-bed of righteousness,
  and peacemakers will reap its harvest.

Happy is the one whose delight is to meditate on the law of the Lord;
  he is like a tree planted by a stream of water,
    yielding its fruit in due season, foliage never fading.

But the godless say to themselves, 'Let us set a trap for the just man,
  who claims that he knows God.'
Blinded by their own malevolence, they fail to see God's hidden plan,
  never thinking that innocence will have its reward.

Jesus taught his disciples that he would be killed and rise again,
  but they did not understand, and were afraid to ask.
Jesus, knowing their interest was only in who was the greatest, said,
  'If anyone wants to be first, he must make himself last of all.'
    'Whoever receives a child like this in my name receives me.'

Proper 21

The Sunday between 25 September and 1 October inclusive.

Continuous: Esther 7:1–6, 9–10; 9:20–22; Psalm 124; *or Related:* Numbers 11:4–6, 10–16, 24–29; Psalm 19:7–14;
James 5:13–20; Mark 9:38–50.

Lord in times of trial and conflict,
  if you had not been on our side
    we could have been swallowed alive,
    the flood could have swept us away,
    raging waters could have overwhelmed us.

Two days in every year the Jews remember with feasting
  the respite they had from their enemies,
    when Queen Esther persuaded the king
      to spare her life and the lives of her people.

How different from the lamentations of the Israelites in the desert,
  greedy for better things, their appetites quite gone,
    seeing nothing but manna wherever they looked.
Moses was troubled, found the whole people too heavy a burden,
  and obeyed the command to call out seventy elders.
Sharing in his spirit, they were seized by prophetic ecstasy,
  confirming the power of God to the people.

If any one of us is in trouble, let us pray,
if any one of us is in good heart, let him sing praises,
if any one of us is ill, let us call the elders of the church,
  and pray and anoint him in the name of the Lord.

Some who call in the name of the Lord are not one with us,
and we are tempted to rebuke them,
    but Jesus had the answer when he told his disciples,
      'He who is not against us is on our side.'

Grant that we attend to our own shortcomings,
  removing from our being things that cause offence,
    and learning to live at peace with one another.

Proper 22

The Sunday between 2 and 8 October inclusive.

Continuous: Job 1:1; 2:1–10; Psalm 26; *or Related:* Genesis 2:18–24; Psalm 8; Hebrews 1:1–4; 2:5–12; Mark 10:2–16.

Lord of continuing revelation,
  you spoke in many and varied ways through your prophets,
    and you spoke to us in Jesus, the radiant reflection of your glory.

It was fitting that you should make perfect through suffering
  the pioneer of our salvation,
    for he does not shrink from calling men his brothers,
      and suffering is the lot of mankind.

The story of Job teaches us much about trust in adversity,
  holding fast to integrity, when ruined without a cause,
    for if we accept good from God,
      shall we not also accept the bad,
        since that is the way the world is made?

Uphold the cause of the good who put unfaltering trust in you,
  and let their feet be planted on firm ground.

Today's scientific story of creation is different from that in Genesis,
  but the divine truths are still the same.
Male and female evolved together,
  procreating by becoming one flesh,
and recognizing more and more
  that it is not good for one person to be alone,
    nor for married people to separate.
As Jesus said, 'It was because of stubborn hardness of heart
  that Moses allowed a certificate of dismissal.
    Whoever divorces and remarries commits adultery.
      What God has joined together let no one separate.'
Are all joined by God? Are there occasions for loving mercy?

Spare us from the greater of two evils.

Proper 23

The Sunday between 9 and 15 October inclusive.

Continuous: Job 23:1–9, 16–17; Psalm 22:1–15; *or Related:* Amos 5:6–7, 10–15; Psalm 90:12–17;
Hebrews 4:12–16; Mark 10:17–31.

Lord of the mystery of suffering,
    there are those who cry, 'Why have you forsaken me?'
      and there is no answer by day, nor respite by night.

The story of Job tells how he sought you north, south, east and west,
    to test out his arguments in full, and did not find you.
      He was faint-hearted and filled with fear,
        yet not reduced to silence by the darkness.

The Psalmist felt abused and scorned by everyone,
    his strength draining away like water, his heart melting within him,
    his mouth dry as a potsherd, his soul laid low in the dust of death.

There are those who deserve the rewards of justice,
    those who trample on the poor, and abhor the speaker of truth,
      those who bully the innocent, and extort ransoms,
        and in court push the destitute out of the way.
Their fate will be that they will build houses of hewn stone,
    but will not live in them,
      they will plant pleasant vineyards,
        but will not drink their wine.

Teach us, Lord, to count our days, that our minds may learn wisdom.
    Satisfy us at daybreak with your love,
      that we may sing for joy and be glad all our days.

The word of God cuts more keenly than any two-edged sword,
    discriminating among the thoughts and intentions of our hearts.

In Jesus we have a high priest able to sympathize with our weaknesses,
    for he was tested in every respect as we are, yet without sin.
      Grant us grace to be one with Jesus.

Proper 24

The Sunday between 16 and 22 October inclusive.

Continuous: Job 38:1−7, [34−41]; Psalm 104:1−9, 24, 35c (*or* Psalm 104:1−9); *or Related:* Isaiah 53:4−12; Psalm 91:9−16; Hebrews 5:1−10; Mark 10:35−45.

Lord of the inspiration of prophets, and of the writers of psalms,

How perceptively they wrote of the significance of suffering,
    and of its effectiveness in healing the wounds of sin.
How accurately they foreshadowed the response of Jesus,
    maltreated, yet he was submissive, and did not open his mouth.

Like every high priest chosen from among mortals,
    he was appointed our representative before God.
He was able to bear patiently with the ignorant and erring
    since he too was beset with weakness.
He learned obedience through his sufferings,
    and became the source of eternal salvation for all who obey him.

James and John revealed their selfish ambitions by asking
    to sit with Jesus in glory at his right hand and left.
He replied, 'You do not understand what you are asking,'
    'Can you drink the cup that I drink?' They replied, 'We can.'
To our surprise, he agreed, adding,
    'But to sit on my right and left is not for me to grant.
      It has already been assigned.'

The other disciples were angry and he addressed them all,
    sensing that others among them wished to be great,
      telling them that each must become the other's servant,
'For the Son of Man came not to be served but to serve,
    and to give his life, a ransom for many.'

Grant us, Lord, a share of your patience,
    of your understanding and forbearance,
      and strength and health to share your cup.

Proper 25

The Sunday between 23 and 29 October inclusive.

Continuous: Job 42:1–6, 10–17; Psalm 34:1–8, 19–22 (*or* Psalm 34:1–8);
or Related: Jeremiah 31:7–9; Psalm 126;
Hebrews 7:23–28; Mark 10:46–52.

Lord, the preserver of the remnant of Israel,
   you brought them home, weeping as they came,
      and smoothed their paths so that they did not stumble.

They were like people renewed in health,
   those who sowed in tears did reap with songs of joy,
      and among the nations it was said,
         'The Lord has done great things for them.'

Many are the afflictions of the righteous,
   but you, Lord, rescue them from each and every one.

Job, after much suffering and complaining,
   had spoken of things that he had not understood.
He knew God only by report,
   but when he saw him with his own eyes
      he despised himself, repenting in dust and ashes,
and the end of his life was blessed more than the beginning.

May we taste and see that you, Lord, are good,
   and may we be happy as we find our refuge in you.

We recognize in Jesus a perpetual priesthood,
   always alive to plead on behalf of those
      who approach God through him.
He has no need to offer sacrifices daily,
   for he did this once and for all when he offered himself.

Grant that we may realise how spiritually blind we have become
      and ask, 'Lord, I want my sight back.'
And may the reply be 'Go, your faith has healed you,'
   so that we may follow Jesus on the way.

Bible Sunday

Isaiah 55:1–11; Psalm 19:7–14; 2 Timothy 3:14 – 4:5; John 5:36b–47.

Lord of the sacred writings,
   familiar to many of us from our childhood,
      with power to make us wise,
         and to lead to salvation through Christ Jesus,

Grant that we may stand by the truths
   that we have learned and firmly believed,
knowing that all inspired Scripture teaches the truth and refutes error,
   and has its use for reformation of manners,
      and discipline in right living.

May we faithfully proclaim the message, and press it home,
      using argument, reproof and appeal,
         with all the patience that teaching requires.

Make us wary of people rejecting sound teaching,
   each following their own whim,
      and finding teachers to tickle their fancy.

The Jews studied the Scriptures diligently,
   supposing that in them they had eternal life,
      yet refused to come to Jesus,
         to whom the testimony of Scripture pointed.

They accepted honour from one another,
   and cared nothing for the honour that comes from God.
How could they believe Moses and yet not believe Jesus,
      for it was of Jesus that Moses wrote?

May we seek the Lord while he may be found,
   and call upon him while he is near.

May the wicked abandon their ways and return to the Lord,
   for God's thoughts are not our thoughts,
      nor are his ways our ways.

Yet by your grace we can draw near to you,
   and the Spirit of truth can speak to us.

Dedication Festival

The First Sunday in October or the Last Sunday after Trinity.

Genesis 28:11–18 (*or* Revelation 21:9–14); Psalm 122; 1 Peter 2:1–10;
John 10:22–29.

Lord of the sacred pillar set up by Jacob,
   the stone pillow on which he dreamed,
      and saw a ladder from ground to heaven, a highway for angels,

Awaking, awestruck, he declared,
   'This is none other than the House of God,'
     so he called that place Bethel,
       a place for rejoicing with prayer for Jerusalem:
         'Peace be within your walls, and prosperity in your palaces.'

You, Lord, are the living stone,
   rejected by mortals but chosen by God,
and we, as living stones, must be built up into a spiritual house
   to form a holy priesthood to offer spiritual sacrifices.

For those who have no faith,
   Christ, the stone rejected, has become a stone to trip over,
     a rock to stumble against, because they refuse to believe the word.

You declare us to be a chosen race, a royal priesthood,
   a dedicated nation, a people claimed by God for his own,
for God has called us out of darkness into his marvellous light.

Therefore we must put away all wickedness,
   deceit, hypocrisy, jealousy, malicious talk of every kind,
     and crave for pure spiritual milk, like new-born infants.

It was at the Dedication Festival in Jerusalem that the Jews asked,
   'How long are you going to keep us in suspense?
    Tell us plainly – are you the Messiah?'
And you answered plainly, 'I have told you, and you do not believe.
   My deeds in the Father's name are my credentials.
    No one can snatch my sheep out of the Father's care.'

And thereby you dedicated us as your spiritual temple, your Church.

All Saints' Day

The Sunday between 30 October and 5 November or, if this is not kept as All Saints' Sunday, on 1 November itself.

Wisdom 3:1–9 (*or* Isaiah 25:6–9); Psalm 24:1–6; Revelation 21:1–6a; John 11:32–44.

Lord of every living soul, and of the departed,
    we know that the souls of the just are in your hand.

In the eyes of the foolish their departure was reckoned as defeat,
   and their going from us as disaster,
      but they are at peace, and have a sure hope of immortality.

Those who have put their trust in you know that you are true,
   and the faithful will attend upon you in love,
      for they are your chosen, and grace and mercy will be theirs.

The veil of death shrouding all the peoples will be destroyed,
   tears will be wiped away from every face,
      and there will be rejoicing in their salvation.
For these are they who have clean hands and pure hearts,
   who have not set their minds on what is false,
      or sworn deceitfully.

May our vision be like theirs, a vision of a new heaven
   and a new earth, the new Jerusalem, the Holy City,
      made ready like a bride adorned for her husband,
         where God has his dwelling with mortals.

Jesus gave us a foretaste of these things bringing Lazarus to life.
   In the context of a loving family, weeping their distress,
      he was greatly disturbed in his spirit, and he too wept.

May we heed his word: 'Did I not tell you that if you have faith
   you will see the glory of God?'
It was for the benefit of the crowd standing there that he said it,
   so that they might believe he was sent from the Father
      when they saw Lazarus alive and well.

The Fourth Sunday before Advent

This is Proper 26 Alternative in RCL. The Sunday between 30 October and 5 November inclusive.

For use if the feast of All Saints was celebrated on 1 November and alternative propers are needed.

Deuteronomy 6:1–9; Psalm 119:1–8; Hebrews 9:11–14; Mark 12:28–34.

Lord of all those who conform to your law,
  who set their hearts on finding you,
    and have lived according to your will,
      praising you in sincerity of heart,

As the perceptive scribe recognized, the first of the commandments is:
  'The Lord our God is the one Lord,
    and we must love the Lord our God
      with all our heart, with all our soul,
        with all our mind, and with all our strength.'
And the second is this: 'We must love our neighbour as ourself.'

The scribe responded, 'Well said, Teacher,' and added,
  'Obeying these commandments means far more than
    any whole offerings and sacrifices.'
Jesus saw how thoughtfully he answered and told him,
  'You are not far from the kingdom of God.'

Grant, Lord, that we may recite these commandments to our children,
  talk about them indoors and out of doors,
    when we lie down and when we get up.

In Christ we have the high priest of good things already in being,
  who entered the sanctuary once for all,
    gave his own blood in sacrifice, and secured an eternal liberation,
cleansing our consciences from the deadness of our former ways,
  in order to serve the living God.

To him be praise and glory and thanksgiving.

The Third Sunday before Advent

This is Proper 27 Alternative in RCL. The Sunday between 6 and 12 November inclusive.

Jonah 3:1–5, 10; Psalm 62:5–12; Hebrews 9:24–28; Mark 1:14–20.

Lord of ultimate power
  and unfailing love,

You are our rock of deliverance and a strong tower,
  on you our safety and honour depend.
For you alone our souls wait in silence.

Grant us to trust in you at all times,
    and to pour out our hearts before you,
      and never to let the desire of our hearts be
        the increase of material wealth.

Both common people and people of rank are empty air and a sham,
    so that when placed on the scales they rise,
      all of them are lighter than air.

If they gave up their wicked ways, as did Nineveh,
    and made evident their repentance,
      would you then not inflict the punishment that they deserve?

As Jesus said, 'The time has arrived, the kingdom of God is upon you.
    Repent and believe the gospel.'

He did not choose to make sacrifices according to tradition,
  repeating them year after year with the blood of animals.
He appeared once for all at the climax of history
  to abolish sin by the sacrifice of himself.

Now he has entered a sanctuary not made with human hands,
  he has entered heaven itself.
And when he appears a second time, he will not deal with sin
  but bring salvation to those who eagerly await him.

Grant that when the call comes to us
  to follow Jesus and become fishers of men,
    we may respond at once, putting all our trust in him.

The Second Sunday before Advent

*This is Proper 28 Alternative in RCL. The Sunday between 13 and
19 November inclusive.*

Daniel 12:1−3; Psalm 16; Hebrews 10:11−14, [15−18,] 19−25; Mark
13:1−8.

Lord of the good that we enjoy,
   we are well content with our inheritance,
      you maintain our boundaries in pleasant places.

You have given us good counsel, and we cannot be shaken;
   in the night you have imparted wisdom in our inmost beings,
      therefore our hearts are glad and our spirits rejoice,
         and when we lie down to sleep, we are unafraid.

In your presence is the fullness of joy,
   and at your right hand are pleasures for evermore.

Christ, having offered for all time a single sacrifice for sins,
   sealed his covenant, 'I will set my laws in their hearts
      and write them on their understanding.
         Their sins and wicked deeds I will remember no more.'

Grant that we may make our approach in sincerity of heart,
   and the full assurance of faith,
      inwardly cleansed from a guilty conscience.
Let us be firm and unswerving in the confession of our hope,
   for we can trust you, the giver of the promise,
      and let us see how each of us may best arouse others
         to love and active goodness.

Jesus predicted the destruction of the Temple,
   but knew not the day or the hour.
      'Be on your guard,' he said.
         'Many will come claiming my name.'

May we ever be on our guard,
   aware of the first birth-pangs of the new age,
      knowing that the end is still to come.

Christst the King

This is Proper 29 Alternative in RCL. The Sunday between 20 and 26 November inclusive.

Daniel 7:9–10, 13–14; Psalm 93; Revelation 1:4b–8; John 18:33–37.

Lord of our visions and dreams,
   in which the majesty of human kings is expanded and enriched
      to try to do justice to the greater glory
         of your divine sovereignty,

Daniel saw one like a human being,
   who approached and was presented to the Ancient of Years.

Sovereignty and glory and kingly power were given to him,
   and were never to be destroyed or to pass away.

These visions were strangely compelling previsions
   of your kingship,
      with all nations serving you.

Your kingdom was not of this world,
   and your followers were well aware
      that your kingdom belongs elsewhere.
If they had thought of you as an earthly king,
   they would have fought to release you from the Jews.

Even Pilate called you a king,
   but knew not how to recognize the truth
      to which you bore witness.

We have been made members of a royal house,
   with you, Lord, as sovereign over all,
      ruler of the kings of the earth.

Grant that in our worship we may see you as king,
   ruling our lives through inspiration,
      rich with the grace that marries service with love,
         and time with eternity.

Harvest Thanksgiving

CLC p. 115. RCL: Thanksgiving Day. The fourth Thursday in November (USA) and the second Monday in October (Canada).

Joel 2:21–27; Psalm 126; 1 Timothy 2:1–7 (*or* Timothy 6:6–10); Matthew 6:25–33.

Lord of the blessings that lead to thanksgiving,
   there are the lean years and the fat years,
      and when fortunes are restored
         we are like people renewed in health.

When good things are ravaged by misfortune,
   like attacks by armies of swarming locusts,
      we trust in your deliverance.

Then those who go out weeping, carrying their bags of seed,
   will come back with songs of joy, carrying home their sheaves.
The open pastures will be green, trees will bear fruit,
      the threshing-floors will be heaped with grain,
      the vats will overflow with new wine and oil.

We offer thanksgivings with our prayers, petitions and intercessions,
   especially for sovereigns and those in high office,
      that we may lead a tranquil and quiet life,
         free to practise our religion with dignity.

We pray that all should find salvation and come to know the truth
   that there is one God, and one mediator, Jesus Christ,
      who sacrificed himself to win freedom for all mankind,
         revealing God's purpose at God's good time.

How, then, can we be anxious about what we eat, drink and wear?
   Birds do not sow and reap, but you provide their food.
The lilies do no work and do not spin,
      yet Solomon in all his splendour was not attired like one of these.

It is the ungodly who worry about food, drink and clothes.
   Anxious thought cannot add one day to our span of life,
      and could well lead to one day less.

Thanks be to God for all our blessings, known and unknown.

Lord For All Seasons

Year C

The First Sunday of Advent

Jeremiah 33:14 –16; Psalm 25:1–10; 1 Thessalonians 3:9–13; Luke 21:25–36.

Lord of the promise made to Israel,
   fulfilled in the righteous branch,
      Jesus of the line of David,
         'The Lord is our Righteousness'
           in the name of the New Jerusalem,

To you, Lord, we lift up our souls,
   trusting not to be put to shame
      for wanton treachery,
         as were some of your people.

God of our salvation,
   teach us your paths, and lead us in your truth.

Your steadfast love and faithfulness
   have been known throughout the ages.

Night and day we pray most earnestly
   that you should restore whatever is lacking in our faith.

Strengthen our hearts in holiness,
   that we may be blameless
      at the coming of our Lord Jesus.

When there is distress of nations,
   and fear and foreboding
      of what is coming upon the world,
grant us the grace to recognize
   the coming of the Son of Man
      with power and glory.

Keep us on our guard,
   that our hearts be not weighed down
      by the worries of this life.
Let our trust in you be seen
   in our peace and confidence,
   in our lively joy,
      and in thanksgiving.

The Second Sunday of Advent

Baruch 5:1–9 (*or* Malachi 3:1–4); *Canticle*: Benedictus; Philippians 1:3–11;
Luke 3:1–6.

Lord of the way,
  cleared and trodden by the prophets,
the way prepared by John
  by his baptism of repentance
    for the forgiveness of sins,

Let the mercy you show
  set us free to worship you without fear,
and let your tender compassion
  break upon us, like dawn from on high,
shining on the dwellers in darkness,
  and those overshadowed by death,
that their feet may be guided
  in the way of peace.

Strip off our garments of mourning and sorrow,
and reclothe us in glorious majesty by the beauty of your gifts,
renaming us with the joy of Jerusalem
  'Righteous Peace, Splendour of Godliness'.

Let our prayers be ever joyful,
  thankful for the privilege of sharing
    in the defence of the gospel.

May the love of all your people grow ever richer
  in knowledge and insight of every kind,
enabling us to learn from experience
  what things really matter,
that in the day of completion,
  in the presence of Christ,
    we may be flawless and without blame,
      yielding a full harvest of righteousness.

Make us worthy pilgrims,
  walking boldly in the way of truth,
    full of the fun of a holy life,
      and winning others to your service.

The Third Sunday of Advent

Zephaniah 3:14–20; *Canticle*: Isaiah 12:2–6 (*or* Psalm 146:5–10);
Philippians 4:4–7; Luke 3:7–18.

Lord our deliverer,
   our refuge and defence,
you are ever in our midst,
   rescuing the lost,
    delivering the oppressed,
     and bringing us home.

We rejoice with all our heart;
   no longer do our hands hang limp,
    no longer do we fear disaster.

You are among us in majesty;
   with joy we draw water
    from the wells of deliverance.

Your peace is beyond all understanding,
   and guards our hearts and our thoughts,
delivering us from anxiety
   as we make our requests known to you
    in prayer and petition,
     with thanksgiving.

Help us to prove our repentance
   by the fruits we bear,
    being known to everyone
     for our consideration of others.

What we have of clothing and food
   may we share with those who have not.

Let us never take more than is our due,
   nor bully, nor blackmail,
    nor grumble about our pay,
lest we find ourselves tossed
   in the winnowing-shovel of our consciences,
falling as chaff
   to be consumed with unquenchable fire.

The Fourth Sunday of Advent

Micah 5:2–5a; *Canticle*: Magnificat (*or* Psalm 80:1–7); Hebrews 10:5–10;
Luke 1:39–45, [46–55].

Lord of the inner peace,
  born of surrender to your will,

Throughout the generations
  you have been both God of Hosts, preserving your people,
  and shepherd of Israel, guarding your flock.

When sorrow was their daily bread,
  and copious tears their drink,
when the falsity of their prayers and sacrifices
  made you fume with anger,
you showed mercy and compassion,
  and restored them,
    making your face shine on them.

Mary surrendered her person that your will might be done,
Jesus surrendered his all when he came to do your will,
through whom we are sanctified
  when we identify with him in his self-sacrifice.

In Mary we see divine happiness
  because your promise was fulfilled;
her soul sang out your greatness
  and she rejoiced in you as Saviour;
uplifted from her lowliness,
  all generations count her blessed.

You have done great things for all nations,
  by the power of your holiness.

May we endeavour to make sure
  that the hungry are filled with good things,
  that the rich need nothing more,
  knowing that both are certain of mercy
    when they respond to you with awe.

The First Sunday of Christmas

1 Samuel 2:18–20, 26; Psalm 148:1–14 (*or* Psalm 148:7–14); Colossians 3:12–17; Luke 2:41–52.

Lord of our pilgrimage,
    from our early years to old age and beyond,

Jesus, like Samuel, made pilgrimage
    at the age of twelve
        to the Temple in Jerusalem,
listened to the teachers,
    asked them penetrating questions,
        and surprised them by his intelligence,
            and by his answers.

Mary, his mother, was worried at his absence from the family,
    and did not realise that he was bound to be in his Father's house,
        and did not understand
            what it meant to him.

Through him we have been taught
    to show compassion and kindness,
        humility, gentleness and patience;
to be tolerant with one another and forgiving,
    teaching and instructing one another
        with all the wisdom and richness of the gospel;
and to bind everything together with love,
    singing with gratitude from the heart, in perfect harmony.

We praise you for your creation,
    for the glories of the stars,
    for the majesty of the sun,
    for mountains and hills,
    for rivers and valleys,
    for fire and hail, snow, ice and gales.

In everything may we sense your providence,
    in the mysteries of love and fellowship,
    in the suffering of the sick,
    in the anxieties of broken relationships,
    and in the joys of reconciliation and faithfulness.

The Baptism of Christ

The First Sunday of Epiphany.

Isaiah 43:1–7; Psalm 29; Acts 8:14–17; Luke 3:15–17, 21–22.

Lord of the water of baptism and the fire of inspiration,
   water for cleansing forgiveness,
   fire for the Spirit of the living God,

In the works of your creation we trust that
   the waters will not overwhelm us,
   nor will we be scorched by flames,
     for you have fashioned us
       to be loved and honoured as your own.

Your voice is powerful and full of majesty,
   and gives strength to your people,
    a strength that is blessed with peace.

The mystery of baptism and the gift of the Spirit
   can be so easily overlooked in the drama of ceremony,
and the more we probe the meaning, the more questions arise.

Peter and John prayed for the converts of Samaria,
   already baptized into the name of the Lord Jesus,
    that and nothing more,
and laid their hands on them
   that they might receive the Holy Spirit.

John had known his own unworthiness
   but did not abstain from the baptism of Jesus,
    after all the others had been baptized.

As Jesus prayed, not for forgiveness, but to do your will,
the vision of the Holy Spirit, as a descending dove,
   focused your voice from heaven:
'You are my Son, the Beloved, with you I am well pleased,'

and we ask no more for reasons,
   for Christ is one with you.

The Second Sunday of Epiphany

Isaiah 62:1–5; Psalm 36:5–10; 1 Corinthians 12:1–11; John 2:1–11.

Lord of the victory of Jerusalem
   that shines forth like the sunrise,

Your people were called Forsaken
   and the land Desolate,
but now you say Hephzibah, 'My Delight is in Her',
and you call the land Beulah, 'Married',
     to your great delight.

Frail mortals are filled with your abundance
   and they drink from the rivers of your delights,
     as you continue your saving power
       towards the honest of heart.

Let us not misunderstand the gifts of the Spirit,
   by which we say 'Jesus is Lord.'

Some have the gift of wise speech,
   others can put the deepest knowledge into words,
others have gifts of healing,
   others miraculous powers,
others have the gift of prophecy,
   others can distinguish true spirits from false,
others have the gift of tongues of various kinds,
   others can interpret them.

How great are the varieties of gifts,
   all from the same Spirit,
     and all for the common good.

Grant that we are never enticed or carried away,
   by some impulse or other, towards the dumb idols around us.

Let us rather obey the command, 'Do whatever Jesus tells you,'
   as Mary told the servants at the marriage feast,
and find that you have kept the best wine until last,
   as a blessing on the bride and groom,
     and as a sign revealing your glory.

The Third Sunday of Epiphany

Nehemiah 8:1–3, 5–6, 8–10; Psalm 19:1–14 (*or* Psalm 19:1–6);
1 Corinthians 12:12–31a; Luke 4:14–21.

Lord of our joy,
   which is our strength,

So far as we are capable,
   enlighten our understanding of your Scriptures,
and as we hear them read clearly,
   with their sense made plain,
may they be a cause for rejoicing,
   with heads bowed in worship.

The order in your creation makes the sun to rise each day,
   emerging like a bridegroom from the wedding canopy,
and the whole universe is co-ordinated by your laws,
   each part speaking to another without speech or sound.

Isaiah, anointed with the Spirit, announced good news
   and proclaimed the year of the Lord's favour.
Jesus, having read this in the synagogue, declared,
   'Today, in your hearing, this text has come true.'

The Church is like the Body of Christ,
   a single Body, with many limbs and organs.
No organ, be it foot or hand, ear or eye,
   can say to another, 'I do not need you.'
Frail and less honourable parts are treated with special honour,
   so that all parts might feel the same concern for one another,
     and if one part suffers, all suffer,
     if one part flourishes, all rejoice.

Grant that apostles, prophets and teachers,
   and those with greater or lesser gifts,
     may feel the Spirit of the Lord upon them,
and find your ordinances give joy to the heart, and light to the eyes,
   are more to be desired than gold, even pure gold in plenty,
     and are sweeter than the honey that drips from the honeycomb.

May the words of our mouths, and the meditations of our hearts,
   be acceptable to you, Lord, our rock and our salvation.

The Fourth Sunday of Epiphany

Ezekiel 43:27 – 44:4; Psalm 48; 1 Corinthians 13:1–13; Luke 2:22–40.

Lord of the love
  that tells of your divinity
    and enriches our humanity,

Whatever our spiritual gifts and worthy actions,
  if we have no love, we are nothing.
Love delights in the truth,
  is never boastful, conceited or rude,
    takes no pleasure in the sins of others.
Love is patient and kind,
  is never selfish, irritable or resentful,
    envies no one, and keeps no score of wrongs.
There is no limit to the faith of love,
  nor to its hope, nor to its endurance.
Prophecies, tongues of ecstasy and knowledge are incomplete,
  and will end when the wholeness of all things is revealed.
When I was a child, I spoke, thought and reasoned as a child,
  but when I grew up, I put an end to childish ways.
We see now only puzzling reflections in a mirror,
  but one day we shall see face to face.
There are three things that last for ever:
  faith, hope and love,
    and the greatest of these is love.

Over many generations of your people Israel
  you have revealed yourself as a tower of strength.

You will be our guide for evermore
  with your glory filling the Temple,
    where we meditate on your steadfast love.

Simeon waited patiently in the Temple to see the Lord's Messiah,
  and your promise to him was fulfilled,
    so that he could depart in peace.

May we too see the light revealed to the Gentiles,
  whereby we are liberated from the bonds of our sins,
    present ourselves to the power of your love,
      and bow down in worship.

Proper 1

*The Sunday between 3 and 9 February inclusive (if earlier than the
Second Sunday before Lent).*

Isaiah 6:1–8, [9–13]; Psalm 138; 1 Corinthians 15:1–11; Luke 5:1–11.

Lord of irresistible presence and command,
   'If you say so, we will,'
      as Simon Peter said in putting out into the deep to fish,
        after an unrewarded night.

Two boatloads of fish brought Peter to his knees,
   confessing, 'Go away from me, Lord, for I am a sinful man.'
And your reply was taken as another command,
   'Do not be afraid, from now on you will be catching people,'
      and they left everything and followed you.

For Paul your call was like a sudden abnormal birth,
   and he too fell to his knees,
      because he had persecuted your Church.
By your indwelling grace,
   he worked harder than anyone for your kingdom,
      passing on the tradition that he received,
        evidence of your appearances after your resurrection.

They followed the experience of the prophets,
   for Isaiah said, 'I am a man of unclean lips,'
and it was like a live glowing coal that touched his lips
   with the message, 'Now your guilt is removed,'
      and the response, 'Here I am, send me.'

Then the warning of the difficulties, as true today as then,
   'They have stopped their ears and shut their eyes,
      so that they may not listen nor see,
        nor comprehend with their minds, and turn and be healed.'

When we walk in the midst of trouble,
   make us bold and strong,
      brighten our eyes with hope,
        lighten our hearts with laughter, and carry us on a tide of love.

Proper 2

The Sunday between 10 and 16 February inclusive (if earlier than the Second Sunday before Lent).

Jeremiah 17:5–10; Psalm 1; 1 Corinthians 15:12–20; Luke 6:17–26.

Lord of our confidence,
  you test the mind
    and search the heart.

Grant that our hearts may be never far from you,
  lest we trust in mortals, and be unaware of good when it comes.
Our trust is in you, and our confidence springs from you,
  so that we are like trees planted by the waterside,
    with foliage staying green in the drought,
      never failing to bear fruit.

Happy is he who ignores the advice of the wicked,
  and delights in your law, meditating on it night and day.

Give us such confidence in your resurrection
  that our belief is not found to be null and void,
    nor may our gospel turn out to be false evidence about our God,
when the truth is that Christ was raised to life,
  the first-fruits of the harvest of the dead.

The power of Jesus was physically felt
  by the crowds that pressed to touch him,
    and they were healed.
His message was to turn the world upside down,
  so that the needy, the hungry and those who wept
    were satisfied, and their tears were turned into laughter.

And when believers were hated, excluded and insulted
  because of the Son of Man,
    they rejoiced and danced for joy,
      for their reward was yet to come.

Lord of our confidence,
  let your power and love and grace
    fill our whole being with radiant faith.

Proper 3

The Sunday between 17 and 23 February inclusive (if earlier than the Second Sunday before Lent).

Genesis 45:3–11, 15; Psalm 37:1–11, 39–40 (*or* Psalm 37:1–7);
1 Corinthians 15:35–38, 42–50; Luke 6:27–38.

Lord of our delight,
   when we trust in you and do what is good,
      you grant us our heart's desire.

When we wait patiently for the Lord,
   and do not envy the success of others,
      and do not fret or show anger – for it leads to evil –
         then shall we possess the kingdom
            that you have prepared for us.

You have taught us to love our enemies,
   and pray for those who treat us spitefully, turning the other cheek,
and treating others as we would like them to treat us.

For if we do good only to those who do good to us,
   and love only those who love us, what credit is that to us?
      Even sinners do as much.

Let us not judge or condemn,
   that we be not ourselves judged or condemned,
      but let us be compassionate and grant pardon.

If we give, gifts will be given to us in good measure,
      pressed and shaken down and running over into our lap,
for whatever measure we give will be the measure we get back.

We possess a physical body,
but in the resurrection of the dead
   we shall be raised a spiritual body,
      imperishable, and not of flesh and blood.

Stimulate our imaginations, open our souls to the mysteries of faith,
   enliven our worship in silent prayer,
      and speak to our deepest needs.

The Second Sunday before Lent

Genesis 2:4b–9, 15–25; Psalm 65; Revelation 4; Luke 8:22–25.

Lord of the universe,
  Creator, Sustainer, Saviour,

Throughout the generations
  each human being has asked the questions,
    'Who made me?' 'Why am I here?'
and although the answers were for millennia the same,
  the stories told with them varied enormously.

Today the dominant story of how we were made
  is that discovered by scientists,
    from so-called Big Bang, through evolution,
      to continuing creation today,
but the divine truths of creation are ever the same.

Guide us as we meet those who believe other stories,
  especially those whose literal reading of Genesis
    leads to conflicting beliefs about mankind,
      particularly the origin of death,
      the awareness of imperfection,
      and the relation of men to women.

Yet we can all put our trust in you,
  for you care for the earth and make it fruitful,
    and from the gateways of the morning and evening
      the valleys and the hills are alive with songs and shouts of joy.

Our visions of your throne,
  and of the kingdom of the world to come,
    may vary in their form and detail,
but all assert your glory, your justice, your mercy, and your holiness,
  as sovereign Lord of all.

Grant us humility concerning what we do not know,
  and increase our faith in your power to overcome evil,
    and to rebuke the turbulence in our souls
      when we fear we are sinking,
so that we become deeply thankful for all your blessings.

RCL: Eighth Sunday after the Epiphany

The equivalent of the Second Sunday before Lent of CLC.

Sirach 27:4−7 (*or* Isaiah 55:10−13); Psalm 92:1−4, 12−15; 1 Corinthians 15:51−58; Luke 6:39−49.

Lord of the persuasive parable,
  of one blind person guiding another
    until they both fall into the ditch,
  and of the person with a plank in his eye
    trying to remove a speck in another's eye
      without first removing the plank from his own,

When we call upon you, 'Lord, Lord,'
  may we do whatever you tell us to do,
    like the person building a house,
      who digs deep to lay foundations on the rock,
       and the river in flood can not shift that house,
and may we not be like one who hears and does not act,
  who builds on soil without foundations,
    and the bursting river makes that house collapse.

Your word is like rain that falls and waters the earth,
  producing grain for sowing, and bread to eat,
for your word will not return to you empty
  without accomplishing your purpose.
It is good to give thanks to you, Lord,
  to declare your love in the morning,
  and your faithfulness every night.

The expression of a person's thoughts reveals his character,
  for it is in argument and debate that a person's faults show up,
    like the faults in the work of the potter in the heat of the kiln.

Preserve us until you unfold the mystery at the last trumpet call,
  when we all shall be changed in the twinkling of an eye,
    mortality reclothed with immortality,
    perishable body made imperishable.
'O Death, where is your victory? O Death, where is your sting?'

The Sunday Next before Lent

Exodus 34:29–35; Psalm 99; 2 Corinthians 3:12 – 4:2; Luke 9:28–36, [37–43].

Lord of the covenant,
　　commands carved in two stone tablets
　　　　for Moses to convey to the people,
　　　　　　with a veil to cover his face,
　　　　　　　　radiant from talking to God,

The people trembled at your kingship,
　　and when they called on your name you answered them,
　　　　calling them to account for their misdeeds,
and in mercy you proved to them that you are a forgiving God.

But the people could not see the glory of the old covenant,
　　because it too was veiled
　　　　by the stubbornness of their closed minds,
until Christ came to set the veil aside
　　whenever the reader turned to the Lord,
　　　　for where the Spirit is, there is freedom and liberty.

And through the power of the Spirit
　　we are being transformed into his likeness,
　　　　with ever-increasing glory,
renouncing deeds that people hide for very shame,
　　neither distorting the word of God nor practising cunning,
but declaring the truth openly
　　to the consciences of our fellow men.

Jesus went up a mountain to pray
　　and the three disciples saw his face change
　　　　as he talked to Moses and Elijah,
and a voice spoke in the shadow of a cloud,
　　'This is my Son, my Chosen, listen to him.'

Grant us, Lord, persistence in listening,
　　that we may never lose heart in our witnessing,
　　　　and may both sense and convey the awe of your glory,
　　　　　　in the fullness of revelation through a lifted veil.

The First Sunday of Lent

Deuteronomy 26:1–11; Psalm 91:1–2, 9–16 (*or* Psalm 91:1–11); Romans 10:8b–13; Luke 4:1–13.

Lord of all,
   our refuge and fortress,
     the God in whom we put our trust,

Your people remembered how you cared for them
   throughout long ages.
Their ancestors were wandering Aramaeans
   who went down to Egypt and became a great nation,
where they were treated harshly and cruelly
   until you led them out with a terrifying display of power
and gave them a land flowing with milk and honey.

They did not fear the terrors of the night,
   nor the dangers of the day,
for they knew that you had commanded angels
   to guard them wherever they went,
     and to rescue them in trouble.

Now we know that if 'Jesus is Lord' is on our lips,
   and faith in the resurrection is in our hearts,
     then we shall find salvation.

Our Lord is Lord of all, has riches enough for all,
and everyone who calls on the name of the Lord will be saved.

Grant that we may learn from the temptations of Jesus,
   during forty days in the wilderness,
     led by the Spirit, but nevertheless besieged by evil thoughts
      testing his motives.

Stone to bread would have exposed selfishness,
   paying homage to imagined power and authority
     would have been to worship evil,
jumping from the Temple would have been showing off,
   misusing divine power reserved for greater works,
     and for victories over future encounters with evil.

Lord, in your mercy, strengthen us when we are tempted.

The Second Sunday of Lent

Genesis 15:1–12, 17–18; Psalm 27; Philippians 3:17 – 4:1; Luke 13:31–35.

Lord of determination,
   facing the certain death awaiting you in Jerusalem,
the city that murdered prophets and stoned messengers from God,
the city where you often longed to gather your children,
   as a hen gathers her brood under her wings,
     but your children would not let you,

Keep us determined to follow your example
   as citizens of your kingdom,
avoiding the destruction facing enemies of the cross,
   who make appetite their god,
     and take pride in what should be their shame,
       setting their minds on earthly things.

Abram heard you declare in a vision,
   'Do not be afraid, I am your shield,'
and you promised him a child of his own body,
   and descendants as numerous as the stars in the sky.

When you also promised him a land to occupy as his possession,
   he asked, like people of every age, 'Lord God, how can I be sure?'
and there was no answer, other than to obey your commands
   with the faith that was reckoned to him as righteousness.

We are bidden by our hearts to seek your presence,
   and to dwell in your house all the days of our lives,
     beholding beauty with our eyes and inquiring with our minds.

Teach us your way, Lord,
   and lead us by a level path to escape our foes.

Give us patience to wait, Lord,
   that we may be strong and determined
     and put our hope in you,
and that we may be transfigured, at the last,
   from our humble, mortal bodies
     to a form like that of your glorious body.

The Third Sunday of Lent

Isaiah 55:1–9; Psalm 63:1–8; 1 Corinthians 10:1–13; Luke 13:1–9.

Lord of thoughts that are higher than our thoughts,
    and of ways that are higher than ours,
you are ever prepared to take pity and to forgive the wicked
  that abandon their evil ways and thoughts.

There are those who seek you eagerly while you may be found,
  with hearts that thirst for you,
    their wasted bodies longing for you.

Your unfailing love restores them to life,
  they feel satisfied as after a rich feast,
    and there are shouts of praise on their lips.

They call you to mind on their beds,
  and meditate on you in the night watches,
    feeling safe in the shadow of your wings.

We remember past generations,
  all of those who escaped from Egypt,
    who were baptized into Moses, in cloud and sea,
    who ate supernatural food and drink.
All the things that happened to them were symbolic,
  recorded as a warning for us.

Grant that we may never put you to the test,
  or grumble as they did.
You never test us beyond our powers,
  for you always provide a way out,
    and no testing happens to us
      that is not common to everyone.

Trees that bear no fruit for several years are cut down,
  but gardeners are merciful when you want to use your axe,
    and beg you to give the tree another chance,
      with careful feeding and tending.

Give grace to help us to repent and bear fruit,
  lest we all are felled by our faithlessness.

The Fourth Sunday of Lent

Joshua 5:9–12; Psalm 32; 2 Corinthians 5:16–21; Luke 15:1–3, 11b–32.

Lord of the way, the truth and the life,
  prepared for anyone united to Christ,

We once knew Christ from a human point of view,
  but now worldly standards have ceased to count,
    for God has reconciled us to himself through Christ,
      and we are therefore Christ's ambassadors.

You made Christ one with human sinfulness,
  so that in him we might be made one
    with the righteousness of God,
      and be entrusted with the message of reconciliation.

We live in a promised land,
  feasting on the produce of a new country,
    no longer dependent on travellers' fare.

Grant that we may pray with faithful and honest hearts
  in the hour of our anxiety and distress,
    and let there be no deceit in our souls,
nor let us behave like a horse or a mule,
  lacking in understanding,
    whose mettle must be curbed by bit and bridle.

Welcome us to your table,
  to join with sinners and your friends,
    and to learn what it is to be forgiven
      when we repent of our dissolute living.

When there is a spiritual famine in our surroundings,
  and we are far from home and in need of the means to survive,
    bring us to our senses.

Give us the grace to say, 'I have sinned against God,
  and against my family and friends,'
knowing that you will welcome us home
  and prepare to celebrate with a feast
    as if we had returned from the dead.

The Fifth Sunday of Lent

Passiontide begins.

Isaiah 43:16–21; Psalm 126; Philippians 3:4b–14; John 12:1–8.

Lord of the deliverance
  of Israel from Egypt
    and of Paul from his persecuting zeal,

Though we are stirred by destruction of chariots and horses,
  extinguished and snuffed out like a wick,
you bid us to stop dwelling on past events
  and brooding over days gone by,
    for you have done something new,
producing ways in the wilderness, and rivers in the barren desert
  where your chosen people can drink.

Those who sowed in tears
  reaped with shouts of joy, carrying home their sheaves.

Paul counted the pride of his former days as so much rubbish,
  a sheer loss, far outweighed by the gain of knowing you, as Lord.

His one desire was to know the power of Christ's resurrection,
  and to share in his sufferings,
    pressing on towards the finishing line,
      in the hope of attaining his own resurrection.

Six days before the Passover Festival,
  knowing what lay ahead in Jerusalem,
    Jesus graced a supper in his honour.
Mary of Magdala bought costly perfume to anoint the feet of Jesus,
  wiping them with her hair, filling the house with fragrance.
Anointing is for a king, and for a burial,
  and Jesus accepted it as a symbol of both,
    costly for Mary, costly for Jesus,
      and in a different way costly for the poor,
        united in the mystery of sacrifice.

May we ever give of our best to those who deserve most,
  and to those who need most, however undeserving.

Easter Day

Acts 10:34–43 (*or* Isaiah 65:17–25); Psalm 118:1–2, 14–24 (*or* Psalm 118:14–24); 1 Corinthians 15:19–26 (*or* Acts 10:34–43); John 20:1–18 (*or* Luke 24:1–12).

Lord of the new creation,
  born in your resurrection,

Isaiah's imagination outstrips the reality,
  yet fails to encompass the totality,
    no weeping or untoward deaths,
    no natural disasters or family misfortune,
    lions eating straw, in the new Jerusalem.

For your kingdom is not measured in things of this life only;
  we need to search not among that which dies
    but seek the glory of the living in your eternal company.

We read of the numbing incomprehension of the apostles,
  when the women reminded them of what Jesus had told them,
of the power of sinful men setting out to destroy him,
  of the expected putting to death,
    and of his confidence that he would rise again.

They considered the story to be nonsense,
  and they would not at first believe,
    returning to their homes, not knowing what to do.

How many there are today who feel the same.
  Yet men and women are still moved by the Spirit,
    and respond to your call,
finding deep conviction in their belief in your resurrection,
    and coming to know the power and glory
      of oneness with you.

Grant that we may renew our sense of absorption
  into your being,
    be purified in our intentions, and repentant when we fail,
so that, believing in our forgiveness,
  we may praise you with thankful hearts,
    and sing with limitless joy.

The Second Sunday of Easter

Acts 5:27–32; Psalm 118:14–29 (or Psalm 150); Revelation 1:4–8; John 20:19–31. (For those who require an Old Testament reading: Exodus 14:10–31; 15:20–21, to be read before the reading from Acts.)

Sovereign Lord of all,
  the Alpha and Omega,
    who was, and is, and is to come,

You brought grace and peace,
  as the faithful witness, the first-born from the dead,
    freed us from sin, and made us a royal house,
      to serve as the priests of God.

Grant that we may ever be bold like Peter,
  obeying God rather than any human authority,
    by the power of the Holy Spirit.

We feel for the doubting Thomases of today,
  enthusiastic observers and experimenters,
    trusting in the 'hands on' approach.
May they yet find faith by an inner sight,
  and be happy to say, 'My Lord and my God.'

You are our strength and defence, and our deliverer,
    leading us through the gates of victory.

You were despised and rejected,
  thrown down like a useless stone,
but you were lifted up to become the main corner-stone,
  on the Lord's day,
    marvellous in our eyes.

Everything that has breath praises you,
  for your acts of power,
    for your surpassing greatness,
to the sound of all manner of instruments,
  trumpet, harp and lyre, tambourines, flute and strings,
    great clashes of cymbals, the rolling urgency of drums.

It is good to give thanks to you, Lord,
  for your love endures for ever.

The Third Sunday of Easter

Acts 9:1–6, [7–20]; Psalm 30; Revelation 5:11–14; John 21:1–19. *(For those who require an Old Testament reading: Zephaniah 3:14–20, to be read before the reading from Acts.)*

Lord of the new way,
  whose followers, both men and women,
    Saul was licensed to arrest in Damascus,

He could not, or would not, answer the question,
  'Saul, Saul, why are you persecuting me?'
    even when illuminated by the flashing light,
but at the discovery that it was Jesus who spoke,
  he knew of his blindness and was led by hand into the city.
Three days later, while he was at prayer,
  he regained his sight and was baptized,
    and filled with the Holy Spirit, and received his charge,
      'You are my chosen instrument,
        to proclaim the gospel to the Gentiles.'
Like the Psalmist, Saul could have said,
  'I feel secure, I can never be shaken,'
    but when you showed your face,
      he too was struck with dismay,
and only by crying to you for help could he be healed;
'Tears may linger at nightfall, but rejoicing comes in the morning.'

There was another rejoicing in the morning,
  after a night of fruitless fishing,
when the disciples, at your command,
  cast their net to starboard and landed a great catch.

Was it lack of expectation, or a changed appearance,
  that prevented them from instantly recognizing you? –
    until the friendly 'Come and have breakfast'
      left them more sure.

Grant, Lord, that we may be able,
  when asked the threefold question, 'Do you love me?'
    to reply like Peter, 'You know we love you,'
and so receive your charge, 'Feed my lambs and my sheep.'

171

The Fourth Sunday of Easter

Acts 9:36–43; Psalm 23; Revelation 7:9–17; John 10:22–30. (*For those who require an Old Testament reading: Genesis 7:1–5, 11–18; 8:6–18; 9:8–13, to be read before the reading from Acts.*)

Lord of your flock,
   both Lamb that was slain,
      and shepherd of those who believe,

With you as shepherd we lack nothing,
   you guide us in the right paths
      to springs of the water of life,
         and in your presence we fear no evil.

Even with enemies round about,
   you spread a table for us, and our cup brims over.

Goodness and love unfailing will follow us all the days of our lives,
   and we shall dwell in your house throughout the years to come.

Those who see visions tell us of a vast throng,
   all races, tribes, nations and languages,
      standing before the throne of Jesus the Lamb,
         with palm branches in their hands, singing
            'Salvation belongs to our God.'

And angels, falling on their faces before the throne, sing
   'Praise and glory and wisdom,
      thanksgiving and honour, power and might,
         be to our God for ever. Amen.'

Those that are robed in white have passed through the great ordeal,
   and God will wipe every tear from their eyes.

How plainly did you, Jesus, tell us that you were Messiah!
   Your deeds in the name of the Father were your credentials
      when you said, 'The Father and I are one.'

Grant that we listen to your voice,
   and flourish in the flock of the believers,
      receiving eternal life,
         with souls that will never perish.

The Fifth Sunday of Easter

Acts 11:1–18; Psalm 148:1–14 (*or Psalm 148:1–6*); Revelation 21:1–6;
John 13:31–35. (*For those who require an Old Testament reading: Baruch 3:9–
15, 32 – 4:4, or Genesis 22:1–18, to be read before the reading from Acts.*)

Lord God of both Jew and Gentile,
 as revealed when the Holy Spirit
  was poured out on the Gentiles that accepted your word.

Yet it was still hard for some strict observers of the law
 to visit and sit at table with uncircumcized men.
Peter's vision of a great sheet lowered from heaven
 full of four-footed beasts, wild animals, reptiles and birds,
  with your threefold call, 'Kill and eat,' evoked the refusal,
'No, Lord, I never eat what is profane and unclean,'
 and received the uncompromising reply,
  'It is not for you to call profane what God counts as clean.'

He soon found himself witnessing to Gentiles,
 and hardly had he begun speaking
  when the Holy Spirit came upon them,
   just as on the apostles at the beginning,
and the doubters were silenced
 and gave praise to you for having granted
  life-giving repentance to the Gentiles also.

The whole of creation praises you, Lord,
 every living creature on the earth,
  from kings and commoners
   to wild animals and all cattle,
    creeping creatures and flying birds.

In a vision of a new heaven and a new earth,
 the Holy City is seen as a bride adorned for her husband,
  and your home is seen among mortals,
   with the Alpha and the Omega making all things new.

May we glorify you, by obeying the new commandment,
 to love one another as Jesus has loved us,
  that everyone may then know that we are his disciples.

173

The Sixth Sunday of Easter

Acts 16:9–15; Psalm 67; Revelation 21:10, 22 – 22:5; John 14:23–29 (*or* John 5:1–9). (*For those who require an Old Testament reading: Ezekiel 37:1–14, to be read before the reading from Acts.*)

Lord of our pilgrimage,
   be with us to show us your way.

May the Spirit of Truth make his home in us,
   and teach us all we need to know
      so that we arrive at the Holy City,
         where the doors are always open.

We read the vision of the new Jerusalem
   where there is no Temple, for you are to be our Temple,
and the river of the water of life, sparkling like crystal,
   flows down the middle of the city's street,
      with a tree of life on either side.

Be gracious to us, and bless us,
   that your way may be known on earth,
      your saving power among all nations.

Anyone who loves you heeds what you say,
   that the word we hear is not yours
      but of the Father who sent you,
         and you and the Father are one.

Peace was your parting gift, your own peace,
   such as the world cannot give,
      setting our troubled hearts at rest, banishing our fears.

At Philippi, on the sabbath,
   Paul went outside the gate, by the riverside,
      thinking there would be a place to pray,
         and found instead a group of willing listeners.
Lydia, a dealer in purple fabric, a worshipper of God,
   opened her heart, was baptized with her household,
      and welcomed Paul to stay at her house.

Grant that we may open our hearts to you,
   and invite pilgrims to stay at our house.

The Seventh Sunday of Easter

The Sunday after Ascension Day.

Acts 16:16–34; Psalm 97; Revelation 22:12–14, 16–17, 20–21; John 17:20–26. (*For those who require an Old Testament reading: Ezekiel 36:24–28, to be read before the reading from Acts.*)

Lord of the glory of righteousness,
   providing a harvest of light for those who hate evil,
      and joy for the upright in heart,

Your prayer for the unity of your disciples,
   and for those who, hearing the disciples, put their faith in you,
      is a pattern for our prayer today.

We too need to be one, with you and with each other,
   that the world might believe
      that you were sent from the Father.

Many are the stories of the power of your name,
   invoked by your disciples to exorcize those possessed by spirits,
      such as the spirit of divination of the slave-girl at Philippi.

She shouted, daily, 'These men are servants of the Most High God,
   and are declaring to you a way of salvation,'
      until Paul was driven to exasperation and the command,
         'In the name of Jesus Christ, come out of her,'
            producing instant results.

Realising their profit from her fortune-telling had been removed,
   her owners caused Paul and Silas to be thrown into prison.
There was an earthquake, doors burst open and fetters unfastened,
   and the jailer would have killed himself
      if Paul had not shouted, 'We are all here, do yourself no harm!'
Trembling with fear, the jailer escorted them out, and said,
   'Sirs, what must I do to be saved?' and Paul replied,
      'Trust in the Lord Jesus, and you will be saved,'
         and he did, and was baptized with his whole household.

Grant that our witness to your power to save
   may lead others to trust and be made whole.

You say you are coming soon. We say, 'Amen. Come, Lord Jesus.'

The Day of Pentecost

Whit Sunday.

Acts 2:1–21 (*or* Genesis 11:1–9); Psalm 104:24–34, 35b (*or* Psalm 104:24–35); Romans 8:14–17 (*or* Acts 2:1–21); John 14:8–17, [25–27]. *The reading from Acts must be used as either the first or second reading.*

Lord of the children of God,
   those that are led by the Spirit of God,
      who received a Spirit of adoption
         enabling us to cry 'Abba, Father,'
for we are children of God, and heirs of God, joint heirs with Christ,
   whose sufferings we must share if we are also to share his glory,

We share his glory in the pouring out of the Holy Spirit,
   and the young shall see visions,
      sons and daughters shall prophesy,
         and the old shall dream dreams
            of what has now been fulfilled.

Help us to discern the divine truths that ancient stories convey,
   even when they exaggerate or misrepresent divine power,
      as in the story of the Tower of Babel.
The story purports to explain the many languages around us,
   and indicates a longing to recover a single language,
      such as was reported at Pentecost.

Grant us such oneness of faith and loving companionship
   that we may see eye to eye with fellow believers,
      whatever tongue we speak.

Anyone who has seen you has seen the Father,
   and the words you speak are those of the Father.

You promised that whoever had faith in you
   would do greater things than you did,
      so that the Father would be glorified in you.

Peace was your parting gift to us, such as the world cannot give.
May you set our troubled hearts at rest, and banish all our fears.

Trinity Sunday

Proverbs 8:1−4, 22−31; Psalm 8; Romans 5:1−5; John 16:12−15.

Lord of wisdom and understanding,
    appealing to all mankind, from every vantage point,

Wisdom was in the beginning, like a master worker,
    at the side of the Creator, his darling and delight,
        while the delight of wisdom was in mankind.

When we look at the stars in their majestic numbers,
    what is there in frail mortals, human beings,
        that you should be mindful of them?
Yet you have made each of us little less than a god,
    with dominion over your works.

Having been justified by faith, we are at peace with God,
    for you have given us access to grace in which we now live,
        exulting in the hope of the divine glory that is to be ours.

We even exult in our present sufferings
    because suffering produces endurance,
        endurance produces character,
            and character produces hope.

Such hope is no fantasy,
    because God's love has flooded our hearts
        through the Holy Spirit he has given us.

There is so much more that you could have told us,
    but the burden would have been too great.
However, the Spirit of truth will guide us into all the truth,
    taking what is yours from the Father
        and making it known to us.

We find you, Lord, one with the Father, and one with the Spirit,
    three in identity, one in unity.

Grant that we may ever listen for the Spirit of Truth,
    especially when over-confident pronouncements are made
        about the nature of your Godhead.

Proper 4

The Sunday between 29 May and 4 June inclusive (if after Trinity Sunday).

Continuous: 1 Kings 18:20–21, [22–29,] 30–39; Psalm 96; *or Related:*
1 Kings 8:22–23, 41–43; Psalm 96:1–9;
Galatians 1:1–12; Luke 7:1–10.

Lord of majesty and splendour,
    might and beauty are in your sanctuary.

Among the nations, you are king,
    and your glory makes the heavens rejoice,
        the earth is glad, fields exult, the sea roars and everything in it,
            and the trees of the forest shout for joy.

Yet the human spirit is weak, inclined to idols and other gods,
    and Elijah, faced with overwhelming numbers following Baal,
        cried, 'How long will you sit on the fence?'

As a show of strength he called for two bulls to be sacrificed,
    but no fire to be provided, except by Baal or God.
Four hundred and fifty prophets invoked Baal
    from morning to noon, to no effect,
        and were taunted by Elijah – 'Maybe he is meditating,
            or he is on a journey, or asleep.'

Elijah prepared the other sacrifice, dousing it with water, and prayed,
'Lord God of Abraham, of Isaac and of Israel, let this people know
    that it is you who brought them back to their allegiance.'
And the fire of the Lord fell, consuming the sacrifice,
    and the people bowed with their faces to the ground and cried,
        'The Lord is indeed God.'

Jesus was astonished by the faith of a centurion, a foreigner,
    greater, he said, than the faith found in Israel,
        and the centurion's prayer was heard, and his servant healed.

May we never belittle the power of your Holy Spirit.

Proper 5

The Sunday between 5 and 11 June inclusive (if after Trinity Sunday).

Continuous: 1 Kings 17:8–16, [17–24]; Psalm 146; *or Related:* 1 Kings
17:17–24; Psalm 30;
Galatians 1:11–24; Luke 7:11–17.

Lord of care and compassion,
   seen in the raising to life by Jesus
      of the son of the widow of Nain,
echoing the restoration of the son of the widow
   that fed Elijah during drought and famine,

The widow, gathering sticks to cook flour and oil
   for her son and herself, expecting then to die,
      saw Elijah as a man of God,
but it required a special faith, a determined hope,
   to use the last of the flour and oil on one day,
      trusting more to be there on the next.

You feed the hungry, and lift up those who are bowed down,
   protect strangers in the land,
      support the fatherless and widows,
         and bring to ruin the course of the wicked.

Make us aware of the danger of saying,
   'I feel secure, I can never be shaken,'
      lest we be struck down with dismay.

You have so often turned our mourning into dancing,
   removed our sackcloth and clothed us with joy.
Truly, weeping may linger at nightfall,
   but rejoicing comes in the morning.

The gospel preached by Paul
   was not seen by him to be of human origin.
He was not aware of being taught the gospel,
   believing he received it through a revelation of Jesus Christ,
      that he might proclaim it to the Gentiles.

Proper 6

The Sunday between 12 and 18 June inclusive (if after Trinity Sunday).

Continuous: 1 Kings 21:1–10, [11–14,] 15–21a; Psalm 5:1–8; *or Related:* 2 Samuel 11:26 – 12:10, 13–15; Psalm 32; Galatians 2:15–21; Luke 7:36 – 8:3.

Lord of mercy
　for those who confess their sins,

David, damned by the prophet Nathan with the accusation,
　'Thou art the man,' deemed worthy of death,
　　confessed, 'I have sinned against the Lord,'
and received the assurance, 'The Lord has put away your sin.'

Consider, Lord, our inmost thoughts
　and heed our cry for help.
Evil can be no guest of yours,
　save when repentance has turned the evil to love.

Teach us what Simon, the Pharisee, knew in his heart,
　that where little has been forgiven, little love is shown.

And the love shown by the immoral woman at Simon's house
　was evidence of many sins forgiven,
　　and of her consideration of the needs of others,
feet washed and dried, kissed, and anointed with costly myrrh,
　symbols of cleansing, loving, and the mystery of mortality,
　　rewarded by 'Your sins are forgiven' and 'Go in peace.'

Help us to realise that no one is justified by the law,
　however scrupulously it is obeyed in letter and spirit.
Our faith is in Jesus, whose life we now live,
　our old selves having been crucified with him.

Purify our belief, deepen our trust,
　establish and enlarge our hope,
and let our love match the fullness of our forgiveness,
　and witness to your unfailing mercy.

Proper 7

The Sunday between 19 and 25 June inclusive (if after Trinity Sunday).

Continuous: 1 Kings 19:1–4, [5–7,] 8–15a; Psalms 42; 43 (*or* Psalm 42, *or* Psalm 43); *or Related:* Isaiah 65:1–9; Psalm 22:19–28; Galatians 3:23–29; Luke 8:26–39.

Lord of light and truth,
   sent to guide us to the joy and delight of your dwelling,

The Psalmist thirsted for you, the living God,
   as a hind longs for running streams.
When people asked him, 'Where is your God?'
   he cried, 'Why have you forgotten me?'
May we, like the Psalmist, have the grace to say,
   'I shall wait for God my deliverer, and him shall I praise.'

Elijah, in the depths of despair, prayed for death,
but the angel of God knew the hunger of his soul
   and said, 'Rise and eat,' preparing him for a demanding journey,
and for an encounter with you in the silence of a still, small voice,
   before he could be sent back to his mission.

Isaiah felt unwanted,
   ready to respond, but no one asked,
   ready to be found, but no one sought him,
taunted by a rebellious people in pursuit of their own devices,
   crouching among the graves, shaming you by their devil worship.

Jesus showed his power over devils,
   healing the man possessed by many,
     reclothing him in his right mind,
and sent him back home to tell what had been done for him.

Grant that we, by faith, become your chosen ones,
   children of God in union with Jesus,
     putting on Christ as a garment.

Proper 8

The Sunday between 26 June and 2 July inclusive.

Continuous: 2 Kings 2:1–2, 6–14; Psalm 77:1–2, 11–20 (*or* Psalm 77:11–20); *or Related:* 1 Kings 19:15–16, 19–21; Psalm 16; Galatians 5:1, 13–25; Luke 9:51–62.

Lord of all the goodness we enjoy,
   of the counsel that you give,
   and of the wisdom imparted to our inmost being,

Show us the path of life,
   and set us free from self-indulgence in our unspiritual nature,
so that we avoid impurity and idolatry,
   quarrels and envy, rage and selfish ambitions,
   dissensions, party intrigues and jealousies.

By the power of your Spirit, grant us a harvest
   of love, joy and peace, patience, kindness and generosity,
   fidelity, gentleness and self-control,
and make us fit to inherit your kingdom.
Elijah granted the request of his successor Elisha
   to kiss his father and mother goodbye
     before going on his mission.

But the urgency to proclaim the kingdom
   was made clear by your refusal to let a promising follower
     say goodbye to his people at home.
'No one who sets his hand to the plough, and then looks back,
   is fit for the kingdom of God.'

You set your face resolutely towards Jerusalem,
   undeterred by rejection by Samaritan villagers,
     rebuking James and John for their suggestion
       to destroy the village with fire from heaven.

Grant us the same determination to finish our course,
   to crucify our lower nature, and to serve one another in love.

Proper 9

The Sunday between 3 and 9 July inclusive.

Continuous: 2 Kings 5:1–14; Psalm 30; *or Related:* Isaiah 66:10–14; Psalm 66:1–9;
Galatians 6:[1–6,] 7–16; Luke 10:1–11, 16–20.

Lord of the new creation,
  author of peace on earth
    since the kingdom of heaven has come upon us,

Guide us as we witness to others,
  for, as ever, the labourers are few,
    and a heavy crop is there to harvest.

Whoever listens to us as we witness to your mercy
  is listening to you, and to the One who sent you.

If we should discover someone doing wrong,
  give us grace gently to set them right,
    and to beware lest we ourselves are tempted.

Help us to examine our own conduct,
  and measure our achievement
    by comparing ourself with ourself,
      and not with anyone else.

We know that everyone reaps what he sows,
  for God is not to be fooled,
seed sown in our unspiritual nature reaps a harvest of corruption,
seed sown in the field of the Spirit reaps a harvest of eternal life.

Let us never tire of doing good,
  spotting every God-given opportunity
    to work for the good of all,
      especially members of the family of the faith.

May you preserve those who mourn,
  as a mother comforts her son,
    and keep our feet from stumbling.

Proper 10

The Sunday between 10 and 16 July inclusive.

Continuous: Amos 7:7–17; Psalm 82; *or Related:* Deuteronomy 30:9–14;
Psalm 25:1–10;
Colossians 1:1–14; Luke 10:25–37.

Lord of the plumb-line
   set against the walls of buildings in Israel,
      to see if they and the people were upright,
        and they were not,

You laid commandments on your people,
   not too difficult to keep, nor beyond their reach,
commandments very near to them,
   on their lips, and in their heart,
      ready to be kept.

And when they and we do your will
   and turn back to you with all our heart and soul,
      you will again rejoice and reward us.

You, Lord, are good and upright,
   teaching sinners the way they should go,
      guiding the humble to right conduct,
        and leading us in your truth.

May we receive from you
   full insight into your will,
      all wisdom, and spiritual understanding,
so that our manner of life may be worthy of you.

May we bear fruit
   in active goodness of every kind,
      and grow in knowledge of God.

Grant us grace to know our neighbours, near and far,
   whatever their race or faith,
and remind us that anyone to whom we can show kindness
   is the neighbour we are bidden to love as ourselves.

Proper 11

The Sunday between 17 and 23 July inclusive.

Continuous: Amos 8:1–12; Psalm 52; *or Related:* Genesis 18:1–10a; Psalm 15; Colossians 1:15–28; Luke 10:38–42.

Lord, do you not care
   for the Marthas of this world,
      who fret and fuss about so many things,
whilst the Marys sit listening to your words?

Surely your 'Martha, Martha' was a gentle answer,
   for one thing is certainly necessary,
      and it was not be taken away from Mary, who chose what was best.

Abraham was the perfect host to the three strangers,
   waiting on them himself, not knowing their import,
      but it was Sarah who responded behind the scenes
         to the 'Quick, quick, bake a cake,'
and they both were blessed with the promise of a babe.

They who dwell on your holy mountain
   lead a blameless life, and do what is right,
   speak the truth from their hearts,
   have no malice on their tongues,
   tell no tales against their neighbour,
   honour those who fear the Lord,
   hold to their oaths even to their own hurt,
   never accept a bribe against the innocent.

You are the head of the Body, the Church, for you were its origin,
   and through you all things were reconciled to God,
so that we may be brought into his presence,
   holy and without blame or blemish.

Yet we must, with your grace, persevere in faith,
   and never be dislodged from the hope of the gospel.

Proper 12

The Sunday between 24 and 30 July inclusive.

Continuous: Hosea 1:2–10; Psalm 85:1–13 (*or* Psalm 85:1–7); *or Related:*
Genesis 18:20–32; Psalm 138;
Colossians 2:6–15, [16–19]; Luke 11:1–13.

Lord of the power of prayer,
   teach us to pray, and when to be persistent,

that asking what is in your name
   we may receive what is good for us,
searching for the truth we may find union with you,
knocking on closed doors we may find them opened.

Make us rooted in you,
   and built up in you, strong in the faith,
our hearts overflowing with thankfulness.

Let no one capture our minds
   with hollow and delusive speculations,
     based on traditions of human teaching.
Allow no one to take us to task
   about what we eat or drink,
   or over the observance of festival or sabbath,
for they are but a shadow of the reality which is yours.

Let us not be taken in by the sort of people
   who go in for self-abasement and angel-worship,
     and access to some visionary world,
for such people, bursting with the futile conceit of worldly minds,
   lose their hold upon the Head that rules the Body.

Use Abraham to teach us how to commune with you,
   and how to persuade ourselves of your mercy.
He pleaded for fifty innocents to save a city,
   then forty-five, forty, thirty, twenty, and finally ten,
     winning by persistence, knowing that you would go and see,
      for you said, 'I must know the truth.'

Proper 13

The Sunday between 31 July and 6 August inclusive.

Continuous: Hosea 11:1–11; Psalm 107:1–9, 43 (*or* Psalm 107:1–9); *or*
Related: Ecclesiastes 1:2, 12–14; 2:18–23; Psalm 49:1–12 (*or* Psalm 49:1–9);
Colossians 3:1–11; Luke 12:13–21.

Lord of all our possessions
  in this world
    and the next,

provide us with a guard
  against greed of every kind.

There are those who see futility and vanity in everything,
  even in the study and exploration of the universe,
    seeing it as a worthless task
      given by you to mortals
        to keep them occupied.

No wonder they give up in despair,
  and find no real enjoyment in living;
    their lifelong activity is pain and vexation to them,
      even at night having no peace of mind.
They think only of their hard-earned wealth,
  to be inherited by someone who did not work for it.

May we never trust in our wealth,
  for one cannot buy one's life,
    the ransom would be too high.

But let us fix our thoughts on things that are above,
  putting to death the things that spoil this earthly life,
    passion, evil desires and lack of generosity,
and the ruthless greed that is nothing less than idolatry,

lest we pile up treasure for ourselves on earth
  and remain paupers in the sight of God.

Proper 14

The Sunday between 7 and 13 August inclusive.

Continuous: Isaiah 1:1, 10–20; Psalm 50:1–8, 22–23 (*or* Psalm 50:1–7); *or*
Related: Genesis 15:1–6; Psalm 33:12–22 (*or* Psalm 33:12–21);
Hebrews 11:1–3, 8–16; Luke 12:32–40.

Lord of our hope,
   made sure by our faith,
      convincing us of realities we do not see.

By faith we understand
   that the universe was made by your command,
      the visible came forth from the invisible.

By faith Abraham obeyed the call to leave his home,
   looking forward to a city with firm foundations,
      whose architect and builder is God,
   looking for a homeland,
   longing for a better country, a heavenly one.

We are commanded to sell our possessions and give to charity,
   and provide instead never-failing treasure in heaven,
      where no thief can get near it, no moth destroy it,
      for where our treasure is, there will our heart be also.

In past ages, countless sacrifices were offered,
   but you made clear that you have no desire
      for the blood of bulls.
You are honoured by a sacrifice of thanksgiving,
   and by those who follow your way,
      the way to the salvation of God.

There can be no argument,
   though our sins be as scarlet they may yet be white as snow.

Make us like people who wait
   for their master's return from a wedding party,
   ready to let him in the moment he arrives and knocks,
      for it will be a time when we least expect him.

Proper 15

The Sunday between 14 and 20 August inclusive.

Continuous: Isaiah 5:1−7; Psalm 80:1−2, 8−19 (*or* Psalm 80:8−19); *or*
Related: Jeremiah 23:23−29; Psalm 82;
Hebrews 11:29 − 12:2; Luke 12:49−56.

Lord of the ebb and flow
    of the fortunes of your chosen people,

Isaiah sang your love song about your beloved's vineyard,
    a vineyard within walls, on a fertile slope,
    a watch-tower and a wine vat, planted with choice red vines,
and all it produced was a crop of wild grapes,
    a symbol of the decadence of Israel,
with the vineyard trampled under foot and derelict,
    overgrown with briars and thorns.

You looked for justice and found bloodshed,
    for righteousness and found cries of distress.
Some called to you to tend their vine,
    to turn to them and grant them new life.

And they knew your reply would be
    'Uphold the cause of the weak and fatherless,
    see right done to the afflicted and destitute,
    save the weak and needy from the clutches of the wicked.'

The message of Jesus divided his hearers,
    families were split, fired by conviction,
        believers united by baptism, made one in the Spirit.

And with this great cloud of witnesses around us
    we must throw off every encumbrance
        and the sin that all too readily restricts us,
and run with resolution the race which lies ahead,
    our eyes fixed on Jesus, the pioneer and perfecter of our faith,
        who endured the cross, ignoring its disgrace.

Proper 16

The Sunday between 21 and 27 August inclusive.

Continuous: Jeremiah 1:4–10; Psalm 71:1–6; *or Related:* Isaiah 58:9b–14;
Psalm 103:1–8;
Hebrews 12:18–29; Luke 13:10–17.

Lord of the prophets,
  the willing and the not so willing,

You chose them before they were born,
  and consecrated them to your service,
    appointing them prophets to the nations.

Jeremiah was uncertain:
  'I am not skilled in speaking, I am only a boy.'
But you promised to put your words into his mouth,
  told him not to be afraid, and gave him authority to declare
    both destruction and rebuilding.

Isaiah promised light to rise out of darkness,
  provided the hearers ceased to pervert justice,
    and gave of their own food to the hungry.

Jesus gave health to the crippled woman,
  but the president of the synagogue was indignant
    noting only that it was done on the sabbath.
'What hypocrites you are!' said Jesus,
  'You water your ox and donkey on the sabbath.'
    His opponents were covered with confusion.
    The mass of the people was delighted.

Grant, Lord, that we may both respect the sabbath,
  and know that it was made for mankind,
    and thereby find joy in your service.

Give us grace to worship you as you would be worshipped,
  with reverence and awe,
blessing your holy name with all our being
  and forgetting none of your many benefits,
for you are gracious, long-suffering and ever faithful.

Proper 17

The Sunday between 28 August and 3 September inclusive.

Continuous: Jeremiah 2:4−13; Psalm 81:1, 10−16 (*or* Psalm 81:1−11); *or*
Related: Ecclesiasticus 10:12−18 (*or* Proverbs 25:6−7); Psalm 112;
Hebrews 13:1−8, 15−16; Luke 14:1, 7−14.

Lord of the humble
  who sit in the lower places and await the call,
    'Come up higher, my friend,'

for everyone who exalts himself will be humbled,
  and whoever humbles himself will be exalted,

and a feast for the poor, lame and blind
  is better than one for the rich,
    for then there is no question of repayment.

Why did the Israelites stray from you, their true God?
  They entered their land and defiled it,
    making loathsome the home that you had given them.
Priests, lawyers, shepherds and prophets all betrayed their vocation.
They rejected you, the fountain of living water,
  and cut for themselves cracked cisterns that hold no water.

Let not our hearts revolt against our Maker,
  for the beginning of pride is to forsake the Lord,
    and persistence in it brings a deluge of depravity.
Pride and anger were not the Creator's design for mankind.

Let us instead love our fellow Christians,
  practising hospitality, for some have entertained angels unawares.
Give us grace to honour marriage, and love our families,
  and not to live by the love of money,
    content with what we have, and sharing what we have with others.

To you, Lord, we offer a sacrifice of praise,
  and whatever we give to others through Jesus Christ, our Lord,
    is a sacrifice pleasing to you,
for you are the same yesterday, today and for ever.

Proper 18

The Sunday between 4 and 10 September inclusive.

Continuous: Jeremiah 18:1−11; Psalm 139:1−6, 13−18 (*or* Psalm 139:1−8);
or Related: Deuteronomy 30:15−20; Psalm 1;
Philemon 1−21; Luke 14:25−33.

Lord of the choice before us,
   life and prosperity
   or death and adversity,

If we love you and conform to your ways,
   then you promise that we shall live and increase,
but if, in our hearts, we turn away and do not listen
   then we shall perish and not enjoy long life.
Inspire us to make our choice your choice,
   strengthen us to make our will your will,
     and give us grace to love as you love us.

You have examined us and you know us,
   at rest, in action, and as discerned in our thoughts.
We are in your hands like potter's clay,
   waiting to be moulded and remoulded to your liking,

for we cannot expect to become your disciples
   unless we are prepared to leave all our possessions,
     withdraw love from our whole family, if needs be,
       and give up our own life in favour of life eternal.

Useless Onesimus, now so useful,
   one-time runaway slave, now a friend,
     was returned to Philemon by Paul,
       much as he would have liked to keep him.
It was the love and faith of Philemon that led to this,
   faith held in common which deepened their understanding
     of all the blessings that belonged to them
      as they were brought closer to Christ.

We praise you, Lord, for you fill us with awe,
   and wonderful you are, and all your works.

Proper 19

The Sunday between 11 and 17 September inclusive.

Continuous: Jeremiah 4:11–12, 22–28; Psalm 14. *or Related:* Exodus 32:7–14;
Psalm 51:1–10;
1 Timothy 1:12–17; Luke 15:1–10.

Lord of inexhaustible patience
   so outstandingly displayed
      in the conversion of Saul to Paul,

He felt that he was dealt with mercifully,
   because his blasphemy, persecution and outrage
      were the result of the ignorance in unbelief.

There is joy among your angels over one sinner that repents,
   and greater joy for one repentant sinner
      than for ninety-nine who do not need to repent.

You were well acquainted with the sins of Israel,
   foolish, senseless children, lacking understanding,
      clever only in wrongdoing.
The impious fool said in his heart, 'There is no God,'
   for all around him were depraved, and no one did good.

It was in the wilderness, behind Moses' back,
   that Israel committed a monstrous act,
      casting a metal image of a bull calf.
They worshipped and sacrificed to it,
   but even then the plea of Moses called forth your patience.

We know well our misdeeds,
   and our sins confront us all the time.
Against you only have we sinned and done what displeases you.

Teach us wisdom in our hearts
   and faithfulness in our inmost being.

Our daily cry is 'Wash me, and I shall be whiter than snow.
   Create a pure heart within me,
      and give me a new and steadfast spirit.'

Proper 20

The Sunday between 18 and 24 September inclusive.

Continuous: Jeremiah 8:18 – 9:1; Psalm 79:1–9; *or Related:* Amos 8:4–7;
Psalm 113;
1 Timothy 2:1–7; Luke 16:1–13.

Lord of forgiveness,
　　how hard it is to be both just and merciful.

On the scale of nations, Israel suffered dreadfully
　　and blamed themselves for their sins,
　　　　believing it was punishment by you.

When they began to repent, they expected you to rescue them.
Jeremiah was wounded by his people's wound.
　　'Why has no new skin grown over their wound?'
With the Temple defiled and Jerusalem in ruins,
　　they cried, 'For your name's sake rescue us and wipe out our sins.'

Yet restoration began with individuals,
　　those who ground the poor, and suppressed the humble in the land,
　　　　giving short measure, and tilting the scales,
　　　　　　thinking only of making profit, even by fraud.

The story of the dishonest manager, squandering his master's property,
　　has an illuminating blend of justice and mercy.
The debtors benefited from forgiveness,
　　the rich man was pleased to clear off bad debts,
　　　　when he could have taken the debtors to court.
The forgiven manager was given a new opportunity to be just,
　　knowing the power of an astute combination of justice with mercy.

Grant us the ability to be trusted in small things,
　　so that we can also be trusted in great,
　　　　convinced that we cannot serve both you and wealth.

We pray for all in high office,
　　that by their actions we may lead a tranquil and quiet life,
　　　　and be free to practise our religion with dignity.

Proper 21

The Sunday between 25 September and 1 October inclusive.

Continuous: Jeremiah 32:1–3a, 6–15; Psalm 91:1–6, 14–16 (*or* Psalm 91:11–16). *or Related:* Amos 6:1a, 4–7; Psalm 146;
1 Timothy 6:6–19; Luke 16:19–31.

Lord of both the rich and the poor,
    who run together the great race of faith to take hold on eternal life,

They need to obey their orders without fault or failure,
    until the appearance of our Lord Jesus Christ,
        which you will bring about in your own good time.

The rich are not to be haughty,
    nor fix their hopes on so uncertain a thing as money.
They are to be rich in well-doing,
    ready to give generously, and to share with others.

We remember that the love of money is a root of all kinds of evil,
    and in pursuit of it some have wandered from the faith.
We brought nothing into this world, and we can take nothing out.
    Religion does yield high dividends,
        but only to those who are content with what they have.

Lazarus had his consolation after his death,
    the rich man perhaps before he died,
but in his torment could think only of Lazarus as a servant
    to be bidden to dip the tip of his finger in water
        to cool a dry and burning tongue.

With what prescience did Abraham reply to the suggestion,
    'If someone from the dead visits them they will repent':
'They will not be convinced even if someone rises from the dead.'

Some of your people felt no grief at the ruin of Israel,
    they lolled on beds inlaid with ivory, drank wine by the bowlful,
        feasted on lambs and stall-fed calves,
            and anointed themselves with the richest of oils.

Preserve us, Lord, from the folly of self-indulgence.

Proper 22

The Sunday between 2 and 8 October inclusive.

Continuous: Lamentations 1:1−6; *Canticle*: Lamentations 3:19−26 (*or* Psalm 137:1−9, *or* Psalm 137:1−6); *or Related:* Habakkuk 1:1−4; 2:1−4; Psalm 37:1−9;
2 Timothy 1:1−14; Luke 17:5−10.

Lord of inexhaustible love, and unfailing compassion,
   your love and compassion are new every morning.

Your people Israel suffered greatly at the hands of their enemies,
   Jerusalem was destroyed, all splendour vanished,
     and they saw their sins as the root cause.
By the rivers of Babylon they sat down and wept,
   as they remembered Zion.
They hung up their lyres on the willow trees,
   when their captors called for one of the songs of Zion.
How could they sing the Lord's song in a foreign land?
   They would rather their right hands should wither away
     than that they should forget Jerusalem.

Grant that we may learn from their experience,
   resolving not to fret because of evil-doers,
     for like the grass, they soon wither.
Instead may we trust in you and wait patiently,
   hoping that you will grant us our heart's desire.

Through the laying on of hands you gave us no cowardly spirit,
   but one of power to inspire love and self-discipline.
We know whom we have trusted, confident of your power
   to keep safe the treasure you have put into our charge.

How hard it is to interpret the overstatements of Jesus!
   How could we increase our faith enough
     to replant a mulberry tree in the sea?

But we learn from Jesus what it is to be a servant,
   deserving no credit or preferential treatment,
     having done no more than our duty, for the sake of the gospel.

Proper 23

The Sunday between 9 and 15 October inclusive.

Continuous: Jeremiah 29:1, 4–7; Psalm 66:1–12; *or Related:* 2 Kings 5:1–3,
7–15c; Psalm 111;
2 Timothy 2:8–15; Luke 17:11–19.

Lord of majesty and splendour,
   your deeds are pondered over by all who delight in them.

Holy and awe-inspiring is your name,
   and in this fear is the beginning of wisdom,
for they who live by the fear of the Lord grow in understanding.

Your people in exile were told to build houses, to plant gardens,
   marry wives and increase, and not to dwindle away,
to pray for the welfare of cities they dwelt in,
   on whom their welfare depended.

Nation after nation came to respect your power,
   as did Naaman after his cleansing from leprosy
     by sevenfold dipping in humble Jordan,
       when he was persuaded to be humble.

How much he had to learn, from the simple faith of a young Israeli girl,
   to rejection by an angry king,
   to invitation by the prophet Elisha,
     who then sent out a messenger instead.
Yet he knew how to be thankful, a foreigner in Israel,
   like only one out of the ten lepers healed by Jesus, also a foreigner.

For preaching the power of the risen Christ
   Paul was fettered like a criminal, but God's word was not fettered.
We are told to trust that if we die with him we shall live with him,
   if we endure we shall reign, if we disown him he will disown us,
     if we are faithless, he remains faithful.
We are solemnly charged to stop wrangling
   and disputing about mere words, for it only ruins those who listen.

Grant us, Lord, grace to learn from the faith of others.

Proper 24

The Sunday between 16 and 22 October inclusive.

Continuous: Jeremiah 31:27–34; Psalm 119:97–104; *or Related:* Genesis 32:22–31; Psalm 121;
2 Timothy 3:14 – 4:5; Luke 18:1–8.

Lord of the new covenant,
   in which you set your law within your people,
      writing it on their hearts, so that all, high and low, knew you,

Those who love your law and study it all day long
   have more insight than their teachers,
      more wisdom than those who are old,
and your promise is sweet to their taste,
   and sweeter on their tongue than honey.

Jacob wrestled all night for a blessing
   and was given a new name, Israel,
      'one who strives with God',
   and thereafter limped with a dislocated hip,
      having sensed you face to face.

All inspired Scripture before the time of Jesus has its use
   for teaching the truth and refuting error,
      for the reformation of manners, and discipline in right living.

We must stand by the truths we have learned,
   proclaiming the message of Jesus,
      using argument, reproof and appeal,
         with all the patience that teaching requires.
For some people will not stand sound teaching
   but will follow their own whim,
      gathering a crowd of teachers to tickle their fancy.

Grant that we may keep our head whatever happens,
   keep on praying, and never lose heart.

Help comes only from you Lord, for you never slumber, never sleep.
May you guard our lives, as we come and go, now and for evermore.

Proper 25

The Sunday between 23 and 29 October inclusive.

Continuous: Joel 2:23–32; Psalm 65:1–13 (*or* Psalm 65:1–8); *or Related:*
Ecclesiasticus 35:12–17 (*or* Jeremiah 14:7–10, 19–22); Psalm 84:1–7;
2 Timothy 4:6–8, 16–18; Luke 18:9–14.

Lord of restoration of the remnant of Israel,
   with recompense for the years that the locust has eaten,
      feeding your people until they are satisfied,

You care for the earth and make it fruitful,
   you enrich and prepare the soil,
      and crown the year with your good gifts,
         meadows clothed with sheep, valleys decked with grain.

Happy are those whose hearts are set on the pilgrim ways,
   their whole being cries out with joy to you, our living God.
Even the sparrow finds a home, and the swallow has her nest,
   rearing broods beside your altars.

You were the hope of Israel, their Saviour in time of trouble.
   Their disloyalties were indeed many,
      straying from your way, wandering where they would.

There is ever a need for an outpouring of your Spirit,
   so that sons and daughters prophesy, old men dream dreams,
   and young men see visions, be they masters or servants.

Make us aware not only of the magnitude of our offences
   but of the manner of true repentance,
      humbling ourselves, ready to be acquitted,
      never despising fellow sinners.

When the hour of our departure approaches
   may we feel that we have run the great race,
      finished the course, and kept the faith,
and are worthy of the crown of righteousness
   awarded to those who set their hearts on the coming of the Lord.

Bible Sunday

Isaiah 45:22–25; Psalm 119:129–136. Romans 15:1–6; Luke 4:16–24.

Lord of the Scriptures,
   written long ago for our instruction,
      that we might be encouraged to maintain our hope
        with perseverance,

Grant us, Lord, source of all perseverance and encouragement,
  that we may agree with one another, after the manner of Christ,
and may with one mind and one voice
  praise you, the God and Father of our Lord Jesus.

May those of us who are strong
   accept as our burden the tender scruples of the weak,
     and not just please ourselves,
each considering our neighbours,
   deciding what is for their good,
     and will build up the common life.

Bring to our imagination the scene in the synagogue
   when Jesus read from Isaiah,
'The Spirit of the Lord is upon me,
   because he has anointed me,
   he has sent me to announce good news to the poor,
   to proclaim release for prisoners,
   and recovery of sight for the blind,
   to let the broken victims go free,
   and to proclaim the year of the Lord's favour,'
adding as he sat down,
   'Today in your hearing this Scripture has come true.'

There was general approval and astonishment
   that words of such grace should fall from his lips.
He expected them to say, 'Physician heal thyself,
   and do miracles here in Nazareth
     just as you did in Capernaum.'

For he knew the truth of the saying,
   'No prophet is recognized in his own country.'

Dedication Festival

The First Sunday in October or the Last Sunday after Trinity.

1 Chronicles 29:6–19; Psalm 122. Ephesians 2:19–22; John 2:13–22.

Lord of greatness, power and glory, splendour and majesty,
   for everything in heaven and on earth is yours,
      yours, Lord, is the kingdom,
         and yours it is to give power and strength to all.

It was David's plan to respond to your greatness
   by providing for the Temple,
      gold, silver, bronze, iron and precious stones.
And the people rejoiced because in the loyalty of their hearts
   they had given willingly, so that David sang,
'All things come from you, and of your own have we given you.'

By the time of Jesus, the Temple precincts were more like a market,
   with dealers in cattle, sheep and pigeons, and money-changers.
With a whip of cords he drove them out,
   upsetting the tables and scattering the coins,
and shouted, 'Do not turn my Father's house into a market!'

Was it the phrase 'my Father's house' that upset the Pharisees,
   and drove them to ask for a sign to justify his action?
      Would a miracle have satisfied them?
How could they possibly understand his reply,
   'Destroy this Temple (meaning his body),
      and in three days I will raise it up again'?

After the resurrection the disciples understood,
   and we now know we are members of your household,
      built on the foundations of the apostles and prophets,
         with Christ himself the corner-stone.
And in him the whole building is bonded together,
   and we are being built into a spiritual dwelling.

Grant, Lord, that we may ever be glad to go to your house.

All Saints' Day

The Sunday between 30 October and 5 November or, if this is not kept as All Saints' Sunday, on 1 November itself.

Daniel 7:1–3, 15–18; Psalm 149; Ephesians 1:11–23; Luke 6:20–31.

Lord of the seal of the promised Holy Spirit,
   a pledge of the inheritance which will be ours
      when you have given freedom to your own people,
         to your glory and praise,

Confer on us the spiritual gifts of wisdom, vision and revelation,
   with the knowledge of you that they bring.

May our inward eyes be enlightened,
   to know what is the hope to which you call us,
      and the vast resources of power open to those who have faith.

The raising of Christ from the dead
   made him head over all things in the Church,
      which is his Body, of which we are members,
         together with all the saints.

There are so many who are in need,
   the hungry, those who weep, and the hated,
      and we, by your grace, and by our deeds,
         can ensure that you bless them.

The rich have had their time of happiness,
   and those well fed and enjoying laughter
      may soon be hungry, and mourn and weep.

You teach us to love our enemies,
   do good to those who hate us,
      and pray for those who treat us spitefully.

When struck, we are to turn the other cheek,
   and when robbed we should not demand restitution,
      always treating others as we would like them to treat us.

It is indeed a counsel of perfection, a training formula for saints.

The Fourth Sunday before Advent

*This is Proper 26 Alternative in RCL. The Sunday between 30
October and 5 November inclusive. For use if the feast of All Saints
was celebrated on 1 November and alternative propers are needed.*

Isaiah 1:10–18; Psalm 32:1–7; 2 Thessalonians 1:1–12; Luke 19:1–10.

Lord of the sinners,
  whom you befriended, and with whom you dined,

Zaccheus, the little man with a big heart, but prepared to cheat,
  climbed a sycamore tree to see what you looked like,
    responded to your call for hospitality, and welcomed you gladly,
and, without being asked, donated half his possessions to charity,
  and promised to repay, four times over, any he had defrauded.

It was for you a sign of salvation in that house,
  for you came to seek and to save what is lost.

For too long, sin had ruled among your people,
  the cities of iniquity did not listen to your teaching,
    trusting in a multitude of sacrifices.
But you had to let them know
  that you had no delight in the blood of bulls, lambs and he-goats,
  and you could not endure solemn idolatrous assemblies.
There was blood on their hands, they were to make themselves clean,
  and if they ceased to do evil, and learned to do good,
    then though their sins were as scarlet
      they might still become as white as snow.

The sap of sinners who moan all day dried up as in a drought,
  but when they acknowledged their sin to you, you forgave them
    and surrounded them with glad cries of deliverance.

Grant that we may keep on increasing our faith,
  and the love we have for each other,
    so that you may count us worthy of our calling,
      to the glory of the name of Jesus.

The Third Sunday before Advent

This is Proper 27 Alternative in RCL. The Sunday between 6 and 12 November inclusive.

Job 19:23−27a; Psalm 17:1−9 (*or* Psalm 17:1−8); 2 Thessalonians 2:1−5, 13−17; Luke 20:27−38.

Lord of the habit of listening,
   bend down your ear to your people
      and hear the prayers from the lips of the innocent.
Guard them like the apple of your eye,
   hide them under the shadow of your wings
      from deadly foes who throng around them.

Job was utterly convinced that you yourself
   would be his defending counsel in court,
      declaring, 'I know that my Avenger lives,'
and wished his words might be written down in a book,
   incized with an iron tool and filled with lead,
      carved in rock as a witness for ever.

The Sadducees, who deny that there is a resurrection,
   tested Jesus with a question concerning seven brothers,
      the first of whom took a wife and died childless.
Moses laid down that the next should marry the widow,
   to provide an heir, but all seven died leaving no children.
      At the resurrection, whose wife is she to be?
He replied, 'Those judged worthy of a place in the other world,
   at the resurrection of the dead, do not marry.
God is not God of the dead but of the living,
   and in his sight all the dead are alive.'

Grant us the grace of common sense about the coming of the Lord,
   so that we do not suddenly lose our heads,
      or become alarmed by any prophetic utterance,
or by any letter purporting to come from an apostle,
   alleging the day of the Lord is already here.

Lord, you have given us such unfailing encouragement, and so sure a hope,
   continue to strengthen us in every good deed and word.

The Second Sunday before Advent

This is Proper 28 Alternative in RCL. The Sunday between 13 and 19 November inclusive.

Malachi 4:1−2a; Psalm 98; 2 Thessalonians 3:6−13; Luke 21:5−19.

Lord of judgement,
  judging the people with equity,

you raise in our minds the question,
  'What will be the signs that the end is near?'

We are told that wars and insurrections are bound to happen first,
  but for generations there have been such wars.
Severe earthquakes, famines and plagues are also foretold,
  but need not be signs, for we have had them for ages.

The persecution of the first Christians, and their imprisonment,
  were particularly evident for many decades,
    and the destruction of the Temple,
the loss of the beauty of its fine stones and ornaments,
  seemed to many to be the inescapable sign of the end.

Being hailed before kings and governors gave opportunities to testify,
  and you promised to provide such words and wisdom
    as no opponent could resist and refute.

Even relations will betray each other, and put some to death,
  but by endurance souls will be saved.

Some early Christians had extremely strong views,
  not always shared in families,
    concerning maintenance for evangelists.
We read of one who, night and day, in toil and drudgery,
  worked for a living rather than be a burden,
    setting an example for others to follow,
      yet knowing he had a right to maintenance.
He held aloof from every Christian that fell into idle habits,
  those who minded everybody's business but their own,
    and he said, 'Anyone who will not work, shall not eat.'

Lord, grant us grace to discern what is right for us and pleasing to you.

Christid the King

This is Proper 29 Alternative in RCL. The Sunday between 20 and 26 November inclusive.

Jeremiah 23:1–6; Psalm 46. Colossians 1:11–20; Luke 23:33–43.

Lord of Righteousness,
  Christ the King of Kings,

you are the righteous branch, springing from David's line,
    the King who will rule wisely,
      maintaining justice and right in the land.

In your glorious might, may you give us ample strength
  to meet with fortitude and patience whatever happens to us.

We give joyful thanks to the Father,
  who rescued us from the domain of darkness,
    and brought us into your kingdom.
You are his beloved Son through whom our release is secured
        and our sins forgiven.

You are the image of the invisible God, existing before all things.
You are the Head of the Body, the Church, and its origin,
  for in you God the Father in all his fullness chose to dwell,
    and through you to reconcile all things to himself,
      making peace through the cross.

The spiritual shepherds of Israel
  let the sheep of the flock scatter and be lost.
God himself gathered the remnant dispersed in many lands,
  and brought them back to their homes
    where they were fruitful and increased.

The inscription on the Cross was, 'This is the King of the Jews',
and two criminals were crucified with you, one on either side,
  one of whom declared, 'This man has done nothing wrong,'
and asked you, 'Jesus, remember me when you come to your throne.'
  You replied, 'Truly, I tell you, today you will be with me in Paradise.'

Grant that we may be worthy members of your kingdom.

Harvest Thanksgiving

CLC p. 115. RCL: Thanksgiving Day. The fourth Thursday in November (USA) and the second Monday in October (Canada).

Deuteronomy 26:1–11; Psalm 100; Philippians 4:4–9 *or* Revelation 14:14–18; John 6:25–35.

Lord of our joy and thanksgiving,
  to whom we bring our first-fruits,
    rejoicing in all the good things
      bestowed by you on our families,
        throughout the ages,

We worship you in gladness,
  entering your presence with joyful songs,
    and with praise and thanksgiving.
Let us rejoice in you through every season,
  but especially at this time.

Grant that we may be known by everyone
  for our gentleness and consideration of others,
    not worrying about anything
      but letting all our requests be made known to God.

Fill our thoughts with all that is true and noble,
  all that is just and pure, lovable and attractive,
    excellent and admirable,
putting into practice the traditions our teachers taught us,
  what we heard and saw in them,
    and the peace of God that they enjoyed.

Draw us into the mysteries of the bread from heaven,
  not the manna of Moses which was perishable,
    but the true bread from heaven,
      the food of eternal life, bringing life to the world.
You are that bread of life,
  we come to you that we may never be hungry,
  we believe in you that we may never be thirsty.

May the peace of God, which is beyond all understanding,
  guard our hearts and minds in Christ Jesus.

Table of dates of the First Sunday after Trinity and corresponding Propers

Year	Sunday cycle	First Sunday after Trinity	Proper
1999	A	6 June	5
2000	B	25 June	7
2001	C	17 June	6
2002	A	2 June	4
2003	B	22 June	7
2004	C	13 June	6
2005	A	29 May	4
2006	B	18 June	6
2007	C	10 June	5
2008	A	25 May	3
2009	B	14 June	6
2010	C	6 June	5
2011	A	26 June	8
2012	B	10 June	5
2013	C	2 June	4
2014	A	22 June	7
2015	B	7 June	5
2016	C	29 May	4
2017	A	18 June	6
2018	B	3 June	4